D1542279

It's So Easy
Family Favorite
Recipes

It's So Easy
Family Favorite
Recipes

by Krista Griffin

Great American Publishers
TOLL-FREE 1.888.854.5954
www.GreatAmericanPublishers.com

Recipe Collection © 2013 by Great American Publishers

ALL RIGHTS RESERVED
All rights reserved, including the right of
reproduction in whole or in part in any form.

Great American Publishers

P. O. Box 1305 • Kosciusko, MS 39090

TOLL-FREE 1.888.854.5954 • www.GreatAmericanPublishers.com

ISBN 978-1-934817-14-8

10 9 8 7 6 5 4

by Krista Griffin

Front cover photos: Oatmeal Cookies p190 © thinkstock / istockphoto / oksana_nazarchuk;
Roast Beef Dinner p104 © istockphoto / William Mahar; Chili Soup p58 © istockphoto / AnjelaGr;
Everyone's Favorite Potato Salad p68 © istockphoto / Rohit Seth

Illustrations: blender, pot © istockphoto / JungleOutThere; measuring cup, bowl, oven mitt, rolling pin,
timer, flour canister, apron, whisk © istockphoto / Carrie Wendel;
backover, p1, p3, p5 © bigstockphoto / Lorelyn Medina

Chapter opening photos: Starters p9 © istockphoto / Anna Ivanova; Meats p93 © istockphoto /
steele2123; desserts p147 © thinkstock / istockphoto / Bottaci

Table of Contents

Preface

When I think of food, I think of family. I think of gathering around the table at Thanksgiving and Christmas. I think of Papaw saying grace before we eat a wonderful meal that looks as if it took hours to prepare.

Being raised in the home of my Grandma Marene (said Mah-reen-ee), I inherited a natural love of cooking by spending hours watching her cook while always asking if I could help. The very second that passion ignited in me is one of my favorite memories. I was just old enough to stand in a chair, and Marene allowed me to help her make biscuits. From that moment forward, I was hooked.

Our home was always full of wonderful aromas to make your stomach growl as soon as you walked through the door. Many of my childhood favorites, such as Tomato Gravy with Biscuits and Fabulous Sweet Potato Pie, are dishes Marene was well known for around our small Mississippi hometown.

I'm so excited to share the foods I once loved as a child, so families everywhere can appreciate these delicious dishes. These are not only favorite recipes from my family, but are recipes that every family can love... recipes that have been and will continue to be passed down and treasured through many generations... recipes that make use of the convenience of package ingredients and quick cooking methods to allow even the busiest moms and dads to feed their family at home.

Never a chore, cooking for my family today is something I love and enjoy. Food is about tradition and sharing recipes is something I enjoy doing with my friends and family. We have created a new generation of family favorites with dishes like, Everyone's Favorite Potato Salad, Dusty's Favorite Chicken Spaghetti, and Buffalo Chicken Dip.

This book is dedicated to Marene and my "Granny" Bobbie. Thank you for always allowing me to help you in the kitchen. Thank you for having patience with me and for making my favorite foods when I asked for them. I will always miss your warm smiles and your great food. Your memories live on in my kitchen.

My appreciation goes out to my publisher and role model Sheila Simmons and my idol and dearest friend Brooke Craig, both of whom were right beside me encouraging me along the way, and to the rest of my friends at Great American, Diane Adams, Pat Ashford, Christy Campbell, Rose Ellis, Tori Kelly, Anita Musgrove, and Jennifer Warren.

As always my love and support comes from my family, Dusty, Madalyn and Christian. A very special "thank you" goes to my mother-in-law, Vicki Thomas. Thank you so much for being there when I needed you and helping me become the cook I am today. To my mother Tammy Peavy, thank you for making me the person I am today.

To my readers, I hope you see much pleasure and many smiles come from these recipes, just as I have. My greatest wish is for this to be a cookbook passed down from one generation to another, just as I hope that one day Madalyn and Christian will grow up with the passion of cooking for their family as I do for them. The heart of a happy home is the kitchen. So enjoy cooking and make it fun!

With love from my kitchen,

Krista Griffin

Krista Griffin

But God demonstrates his own love for us in this: While we were still sinners, Christ died for us.

Romans 5:8 (NIV)

Starters & Sides

Beverages • Appetizers
Breakfast • Bread
Soups • Salads
Vegetables

Chocolate Milk Shake

¼ cup chocolate-flavored syrup

¾ cup milk

3 scoops vanilla ice cream

In a blender, mix syrup and milk for 2 seconds. Add ice cream; blend on low 5 seconds or until smooth.

Christmas Punch

3 cups sugar

2 cups boiling water

2 packs strawberry Kool-Aid mix

1 large can pineapple juice

1 cup lemon juice

In a gallon jug, dissolve sugar in water. Mix in remaining ingredients. Add enough water to fill rest of gallon. Chill.

Christmas is not Christmas without Christmas Punch. It has been a tradition in my family for many years. If you need a great punch for a baby shower or a wedding shower, try Three Juice Punch served in pre-chilled, stemmed glasses.

Three Juice Punch

1 (18-ounce) can pineapple juice

1 (6-ounce) can frozen orange juice

1 (18-ounce) can apple juice

Mix all and chill thoroughly.

Orange Julius

1 (6-ounce) can frozen orange juice

1 cup milk

Vanilla ice cream, as much as you want

¼ cup sugar

½ teaspoon vanilla flavoring

In a blender mix all ingredients for 30 seconds. This makes 3 cups.

istockphoto / photokitchen

Pomegranate Spritzer

For each serving

6 ounces sparkling water or club soda

1 to 2 tablespoons concentrated pomegranate juice

2 teaspoons sugar

Combine club soda, pomegranate juice and sugar in a shaker. Shake well to combine and serve in glass over ice. Additional pomegranate and/or sugar may be used to personal taste.

Pink Party Punch

1 can frozen piña colada concentrate, thawed

1 can frozen orange pineapple juice concentrate, thawed

2 (2-liter) bottles lemon-lime soda

Crushed ice

1 (12-ounce) bag frozen raspberries

Pour thawed concentrates into punch bowl; stir. Using 1 of the empty cans, add 4 cans water; mix well. After this point, no more stirring after adding the ingredients. Add lemon-lime soda. Add enough crushed ice to cool the mixture. Add your frozen raspberries to the top. Punch will be layers of yellows and pinks then mix together as you serve it.

Watermelon Lemonade Slushy

4 cups pureed and strained watermelon

4 cups ice cubes

⅔ cup frozen lemonade concentrate

1 cup cold water

To make watermelon juice, puree watermelon meat (seeds removed) in a blender then strain though a mesh strainer. Measure 4 cups and return to blender. Add ice, lemonade concentrate and water and blend on medium speed until ice breaks down.

Summer Fish Bowl Party Drink

For each serving

Nerds candy

Small fish bowl

2 ounces pineapple juice

2 ounces apple juice

1 ounce cream of coconut

1 cup ice

Blue food coloring

Sprinkle Nerds on bottom of each bowl as "gravel." Blend pineapple juice, apple juice, cream of coconut, ice and a couple drops of blue food coloring in an electric blender at high speed. Pour over Nerds in fish bowl and serve with a straw. Fun!

Aunt Jean's Old-Fashioned Lemonade

2 cups fresh lemon juice

1½ cups sugar

8 cups water

Mix lemon juice, sugar and water in a 2-quart pitcher. Stir until sugar dissolves. Add some lemon slices for decoration.

Jamaican Mudslide

1 cup crushed ice

½ cup pina colada mix

4 ounces rum

1 (16-ounce) Dr Pepper

Pour ice, pina colada mix, and rum into a blender and mix it for 10 minutes, alternating between ice crush, frappe, and mix, or until smooth, with no icy chunks. Pour even amounts into 4 glasses. Pour 4 ounces Dr Pepper into each glass. Serve immediately.

These Jamaican Mudslides are great for New Year's Eve Parties or your next Girl's Night In. You might want to double the recipe or they will be gone fast.

Good 'N Simple Apple Dip

1 (8-ounce) package cream cheese, softened

1 teaspoon vanilla

¼ cup sugar

¾ cup brown sugar

1 cup nuts (optional)

Blend all ingredients together. Chill 1 hour before serving. Serve with sliced apples for dipping.

Pina Colada Fruit Dip

1 (8-ounce) can crushed pineapple

¾ cup milk

1 (3-ounce) package instant coconut pudding mix

½ cup sour cream

Mix well; chill 24 hours. Serve with fresh fruit.

istockphoto / Olga Lyubkina

Tracy's Black Bean Dip

1 (15-ounce) can black beans, drained

1 can whole-kernel corn, drained

1 (16-ounce) bottle Italian dressing

¼ cup chopped green onions

2 cups shredded Cheddar cheese

1 (2.25-ounce) can sliced black olives, drained

Mix all together. Chill. Enjoy with tortilla chips.

bigstockphoto / thegarden

Yes, It's That Easy, Chili Dip

1 (16-ounce) can Hormel chili, with or without beans

¼ cup diced Jalapeños

1 (16-ounce) package Velveeta cheese, cubed

In a crockpot, combine all ingredients heat until cheese melts, stirring often. This is served best with corn chips.

Nacho Dip

1 (8-ounce) package cream cheese, softened

1 (8-ounce) carton sour cream

1 (10½-ounce) can jalapeño bean dip

1 (1.25-ounce) package chili seasoning mix

5 drops hot sauce

2 teaspoons chopped fresh parsley

¼ cup taco sauce

1¼ cup shredded Monterey Jack cheese, divided

½ cups shredded Cheddar cheese

Combine cream cheese and sour cream; beat until smooth. Stir in bean dip, chili seasoning mix, hot sauce, parsley, taco sauce and ¾ cup Monterey Jack cheese. Spoon mixture into a lightly greased 8x12-inch backing dish, top with remaining cheese and ½ cup Monterey Jack cheese and ½ cup Cheddar cheese. Bake at 325° for 15 to 20 minutes. Serve hot with corn chips or tortilla chips.

Spicy Corn Dip

2 (8-ounce) packages cream cheese, softened

1 can whole-kernel corn, drained

¼ cup finely chopped jalapeños

1 (2.25-ounce) can sliced black olives

⅓ cup hot sauce

Combine all ingredients in a crockpot. Cook on medium, stirring occasionally, until cheese is melted and hot. Serve with corn chips.

Mississippi Sin Dip

1 (8-ounce) package cream cheese, softened

1 (4-ounce) carton sour cream

2 cups shredded cheese

½ cup chopped green onion

¾ cup chopped deli-style ham

Dash Tabasco, optional

Garlic salt to taste

Pepper to taste

Dash Worcestershire

1 loaf French bread or 1 loaf Hawaiian bread

Mix all ingredients together except bread. Cut top off bread and set aside. Hull out the loaf of bread. Place cream cheese mixture in bread and replace top. Wrap completely in aluminum foil and place on a cookie sheet. Bake at 350° for 1 hour.

Signature Buffalo Chicken Dip

2 (8-ounce) packages cream cheese, softened

2 (12-ounce) cans white chicken breast, drained

1 cup ranch dressing

⅓ cup hot sauce

2 cups shredded Cheddar cheese

Mix together all ingredients, except Cheddar cheese. Bake at 350° for 20 minutes. Top with shredded cheese and bake another 10 minutes. This is really good with Ritz crackers or corn chips. (Everyone will be asking for this recipe.)

My friends and I can't get enough of my Signature Buffalo Chicken Dip. Everyone who tries it, asks for the recipe. If I show up to a barbecue without it, they send me home.

Oh My! It's Good Bacon Dip

1 cup shredded Cheddar cheese

3 green onions, chopped

½ cup mayonnaise

1 (8-ounce) package cream cheese, softened

Mix all together. Spread into a small oven-safe dish.

Topping

½ cup crushed Ritz crackers

8 strips bacon, cooked and crumbled

Combine crackers and bacon; spread over cheese mixture. Bake at 350°
until hot and bubbly. Serve with snack crackers.

Got Shrinkage? It's an easy fix. Run cold water over your bacon before frying. It will reduce shrinkage by about half. I wonder if that would work on my paycheck?

Broccoli 'N Cheddar Dip

1 (10-ounce) package frozen broccoli

1 package Lipton Recipe Secrets Vegetable Soup Mix

1 (16-ounce) carton sour cream

1 cup shredded Cheddar cheese, divided

Preheat oven at 350°. Thaw and drain broccoli. In a 1-quart casserole dish, combine vegetable soup mix, sour cream, broccoli and ¾ cup cheese. Mix well. Top with remaining ¼ cup cheese. Bake 30 minutes or until heated thoroughly. Serve with fresh vegetables, bread sticks or crackers.

istockphoto

No Cook Ranch & Bacon Dip

1 (16-ounce) carton sour cream

1 (1-ounce) package dry ranch dip mix

2 cups shredded cheese

1 (2.8-ounce) package real bacon pieces

Mix all ingredients together. Serve with corn chips.

Spinach Dip

1 (10-ounce) package frozen spinach

1½ cups sour cream

1 cup mayonnaise

1 package Knorr Dried Vegetable Recipe Mix

3 green onions, chopped fine (optional)

1 loaf Hawaiian bread

Thaw spinach; drain juice (drain well by allowing to sit or squeezing out the juice). In a large bowl, combine spinach, sour cream, mayonnaise, Knorr vegetable soup mix, and green onions. Mix well. Cover and refrigerate 2 hours. Cut center out of Hawaiian bread and pour dip into it. Use bread that was cut from the center for dipping.

This Spinach Dip is great to serve at baby showers, wedding receptions and especially 4th of July parties.

Fresh Tomato Salsa

3 tomatoes, chopped

½ cup finely diced onion

5 serrano chile peppers, chopped fine

½ cup fresh cilantro, chopped fine

1 teaspoon salt

2 teaspoons lime juice

In a medium bowl combine all ingredients. Mix well. Chill 1 hour before serving. Serve with tortilla chips or corn chips.

bigstockphoto / cclapper

Guacamole

3 avocados, peeled and pitted

1 lime, juiced

1 teaspoon salt

½ cup diced onion

3 tablespoons chopped fresh cilantro

2 plum tomatoes, diced

1 teaspoon minced garlic

1 pinch ground cayenne pepper

In a medium bowl, mash avocados with lime juice and salt. Mix in onion, cilantro, tomatoes and garlic. Stir in cayenne pepper. Refrigerate 1 hour before serving.

bigstockphoto / lidi Papp

Just Like Cane's Sauce

¾ cup mayonnaise

¼ cup ketchup

5 tablespoons Worcestershire sauce

¼ teaspoon black pepper

¼ teaspoon garlic powder

Mix all ingredients together. Allow to stand in refrigerator for 24 hours before serving. Serve with your choice of meat or French fries.

This is a great dipping sauce for just about anything. The longer it sits, the better it gets.

Home-Style Cheese Ball

3 (8-ounce) packages cream cheese, softened

5 stalks green onions, chopped fine

1 jar dried beef, chopped fine

1½ teaspoons Accent, no substitutions

1½ teaspoons Worcestershire sauce

Mix all together. Form into a ball. Chill overnight before serving. Serve with your choice of crackers.

As far as my family is concerned, this is the only way to make a cheese ball. Aunt Kristy can't stress enough, "Do not substitute the Accent."

Easy Pimento Cheese

1 (1-pound) block extra sharp Cheddar cheese, shredded

1 large jar pimentos, ½ juice reserved

1½ to 2 cups mayonnaise

Mix cheese and chopped pimentos together until well blended. Stir in mayonnaise. Best if chilled in refrigerator before serving.

My husband makes this for me all the time. It's really simple to make, but it's so good. My daughter Mady is 4 and she loves it too.

istockphoto/ Catherine Murray

Pimento Cheese Spread

1 (2-pound) block Velveeta cheese, cubed

2 cups shredded Cheddar cheese

1 small jar pimentos

2 tablespoons butter

8 eggs, beat well

¾ cup white distilled vinegar

1 cup sugar

Black pepper to taste

Mix both cheeses and pimentos together, set aside. In a medium saucepan, melt butter; stir in eggs, vinegar and sugar over low heat. Cook, stirring frequently, until thick. Add cheese and pimentos; continue to cook and stir until cheese melts. Season with black pepper to taste. This makes a lot. Refrigerate until ready to serve.

Pinwheels

8 (10-inch) tortillas

12 ounces cream cheese, softened

1 (8-ounce) carton sour cream

1 cup shredded Cheddar cheese

3 stalks green onion, chopped

1 (2.25-ounce) can chopped green chiles

Combine all ingredients, except tortillas. Spread a thin layer over each tortilla. Roll up and chill. Slice into pinwheels. Serve with salsa or picante sauce.

Krista's Deviled Eggs

12 hard-boiled eggs, cut in half lengthwise

¾ teaspoon salt

½ teaspoon pepper

½ teaspoon sugar

1 tablespoon vinegar

¼ cup dill pickle relish

1 tablespoon mustard

5 tablespoons mayonnaise

Paprika, optional

Separate egg yellows from whites. Combine yolks with remaining ingredients, except paprika. Mix well. Fill egg whites with mixture. Sprinkle with paprika. Cook in refrigerator before serving.

Deviled Eggs are simple to make, and these are simply the best. My husband asks for these about once a week.

Simple made easier... After draining the hot water off the eggs, Shake the pot back and forth to crack the shells. Cover with ice water. This will cool the eggs faster and the water gets under the broken shells to make peeling super easy.

And even easier... put all the filling ingredients in a zip-lock bag. Squeeze to mix them up well. Then cut one corner and squeeze to fill the eggs.

Oyster Cracker Snack

½ teaspoon garlic powder

1 teaspoon dill weed

**1 (1-ounce) package dry Hidden Valley
Original Ranch Dressing Mix**

1 cup oil

2 (12-ounce) packages oyster crackers

Mix together garlic powder, dill weed, dressing and oil. Pour over crackers, put in container with lid and shake well. Allow to stand ½ hour before serving.

Bacon-Wrapped Sausages

1 pound bacon

1 (16-ounce) package little smoky sausages

1 cup brown sugar

Preheat oven to 350°. Cut bacon into thirds and wrap each strip around a little sausage. Place wrapped sausages on wooden skewers, several to a skewer. Arrange skewers on a baking sheet and sprinkle with brown sugar. Bake until bacon is crisp and brown sugar is melted.

These Bacon-Wrapped Sausages were served at our wedding reception. They are so good, you better make plenty. After our photos were done and we were ready to eat, they were all gone!

Zucchini Crisps

1 pound (about 2 medium) zucchini, sliced (rounds)

¼ cup shredded Parmesan

¼ cup Panko breadcrumbs

1 tablespoon oil

½ teaspoon salt

½ teaspoon pepper

Preheat oven to 400°. Line two baking sheets with foil and spray lightly with vegetable spray. Toss zucchini in oil to coat well. Combine breadcrumbs, Parmesan, salt and pepper in a shallow bowl. Press zucchini rounds into breadcrumb mixture to coat well on both sides. Place in a single layer on baking sheets, sprinkling remaining breadcrumb on top. Bake about 25 minutes, until golden brown. (Do not turn during baking.)
Serve with ranch dressing for dipping.

thinkstock / istockphoto / rbananka

Microwaveable Meatballs

24 frozen cooked Italian meatballs, thawed

½ cup sweet and sour sauce

1 cup barbeque sauce

Place meatballs in a 3-quart microwave safe dish. Cover and microwave on high 3 to 4 minutes. In a separate dish, mix together sweet and sour sauce and barbeque sauce; microwave 3 minutes. Pour over meatballs. Microwave additional 2 minutes; stir.

Mrs. Anita's Sausage Balls

1 pound hot pork sausage

1 pound regular pork sausage

4 cups shredded Cheddar cheese

2 cups Bisquick

Mix together sausage (with your hands) then add cheese. Stir in Bisquick mix. Roll into balls and place on greased cookie pan. Bake at 375° until golden brown.

Candice Malone shared this recipe. She said, they are the most requested recipe at Malone family get-togethers. These sausage balls are really good dipped in spicy brown mustard or yellow mustard.

Laura's Pizza Roll Ups

1 tube crescent rolls

Pepperoni, sliced into circles

1 package mozzarella cheese sticks, cut in half

Pizza sauce

Unroll and separate crescent rolls. Layer pepperoni over each. Place a cheese stick at the end and roll. Bake at 350° as directed on crescent roll package. Serve with pizza sauce for dipping.

Fried Pickles

1 cup flour

¼ teaspoon salt

Black pepper to taste

1 egg

¼ cup milk

Oil

1½ cups hamburger dill pickles, drained

Combine flour, salt and pepper in a bowl. Lightly whip egg and milk in a separate bowl. Heat oil to hot; dip pickles into flour then egg mixture and back to flour. Put in pan (DO NOT CROWD). Fry until golden brown. Drain on paper towels. Eat with ranch dressing.

Dip these Fried Pickles in ranch dressing and let your taste buds do the rest. They are even better than ones you get from the restaurant.

Golden Fried Onion Rings

¾ cup all purpose flour

⅔ cup milk

1 egg

1 tablespoon oil

¼ teaspoon salt

Oil for frying

4 medium onions sliced ¼-inch thick separated into rings

Mix flour, milk, egg, 1 tablespoon oil and salt. Beat until smooth. In a large skillet; heat 1 inch of oil. Using a fork dip onion rings in batter. Fry a few rings at a time 2 to 3 minutes, flipping once. Cook until golden brown. Drain on a paper towel.

istockphoto / Debbismirnoff

Breakfast Burritos

1 pound pork sausage

¼ cup diced jalapeños (optional)

6 eggs, scrambled

2 cups shredded Cheddar cheese, divided

1 package soft shell tortillas

Picante sauce

Brown sausage with jalapeños. Remove sausage to paper towel to drain; reserve drippings in skillet. Scramble eggs in reserved drippings. Stir in 1 cup shredded cheese. Heat tortilla shells, as needed, 1 at a time, in microwave with a wet paper towel placed on top. Layer sausage, egg, cheese and picante sauce in tortilla; fold. Serve immediately.

Ham 'N Cheese Omelet for Two

6 eggs, well beaten

1 tablespoon butter, melted

Salt and pepper to taste

3 slices ham, chopped fine

½ cup shredded cheese

2 tablespoons real bacon pieces

In a large bowl, beat eggs with 1 tablespoon melted butter, salt and pepper. Spray a non-stick skillet with non-stick spray. Pour eggs in skillet and cook over medium heat. On one half of the egg omelet, sprinkle chopped ham. On the other side, sprinkle shredded cheese then top with bacon pieces. Cook about 2 to 3 minutes. With a spatula, fold omelet in ½ then flip once. Cut in ½ and serve. If you like a little kick, include ¼ cup chopped jalapeño peppers with the ham.

Night Before, Sausage Breakfast Casserole

6 slices bread

3 tablespoons butter, softened

1 pound pork sausage

1½ cups shredded Cheddar cheese

6 eggs, beaten

2 cups milk

1 teaspoon salt

Spread ½ teaspoon butter per slice of bread. Put bread in a greased 9x13-inch baking dish; set aside. Brown sausage in skillet; drain. Spoon sausage over bread; top with cheese. In a separate bowl, whip eggs, milk and salt together and pour over cheese. Cover and chill overnight. Remove from refrigerator 15 minutes before baking. Bake uncovered 45 minutes at 350°.

Not sure when you bought the eggs? We've all had this problem. You don't want to make anyone sick, but throwing away good eggs is just wasteful. There is a solution. Fill a bowl or pan with cold water and add some salt. Place the egg in the water. If it sinks to the bottom, it is fresh. If the egg rises to the top, the egg is no good.

Quick Bacon & Egg Sandwiches

5 hard boiled eggs, chopped fine

4 slices bacon, cooked and crumbled

¼ cup mayonnaise

1 tablespoon sweet pickle relish

Salt and pepper to taste

8 slices bread

Mix together first 5 ingredients. Spread 1 or 2 tablespoons onto each slice of bread. Fold in half and cut in the middle. Enjoy.

istockphoto / 101Photo

Breakfast Casserole

1 pound pork sausage

1 cup uncooked grits

1 cup shredded Cheddar cheese

4 eggs, beaten

¾ cups butter, melted

Brown sausage; prepare grits according to package directions. Combine sausage, cooked grits, cheese, eggs and butter. Place in casserole dish and bake at 325° for approximately 1 hour.

Cheesy Grits Casserole

1½ cups uncooked regular grits

½ cup butter or margarine

3 cups shredded medium-sharp Cheddar cheese

Garlic salt to taste

1 tablespoon Worcestershire sauce

2 teaspoons paprika, divided

3 eggs, beaten

Cook grits according to package directions. Add butter and cheese; stir until melted. Add Worcestershire sauce and 1 teaspoon paprika, mixing well. Add a small amount of hot grits to eggs, stirring well (this keeps the eggs from curdling); stir egg mixture into remaining grits. Pour grits into a lightly greased 2-quart baking dish; sprinkle with 1 teaspoon paprika. Cover and refrigerate overnight. Remove from refrigerator 15 minutes before baking. Bake uncovered at 325° for 1 hour.

Blueberry Pancakes

1 egg

1¼ cups milk

2 tablespoons vegetable oil

1¼ cup sifted flour

1 teaspoon sugar

2 teaspoons baking powder

½ teaspoon salt

½ cup blueberries

Beat egg well. Beat in remaining ingredients, except blueberries, in order given; milk, vegetable oil, flour, sugar, baking powder and salt. Fold in blueberries. Bake on a hot griddle. This will make 12 (4-inch) pancakes.

istockphoto

Yummy Macadamia French Toast

4 large eggs, well beaten

¼ teaspoon ground nutmeg

⅓ cup milk

¼ cup sugar

⅔ cup orange juice

½ teaspoon vanilla

1 (1-pound) loaf Italian bread cut in 1-inch slices

⅔ cup melted butter

½ cup chopped macadamia nuts

Mix eggs with nutmeg, milk, sugar, orange juice and vanilla. Stir well. Fit bread slices in a lightly greased 9x13-inch pan. Pour egg mixture over bread slices, cover and refrigerate 8 hours. Turn bread once. Pour butter in a 10x5-inch pan. Place bread slices in a single layer in pan. Bake at 400° for 10 minutes. Sprinkle with nuts. Bake another 10 minutes.

Mayonnaise Biscuits

1 cup self-rising flour

½ cup milk

2 tablespoons mayonnaise

Mix all together. In a treated muffin pan, drop 1 teaspoonful into each cup. Bake at 475° until golden brown, about 10 minutes. Serve hot.

Cheese & Garlic Biscuits

2 cups baking mix

⅔ cup milk

½ cup shredded Cheddar cheese

¼ cup margarine, melted

¼ teaspoon garlic powder

Combine baking mix, milk and cheese in a bowl. Stir constantly for 30 seconds or until soft dough forms. Drop by spoonfuls onto ungreased baking dish. Bake 450° for 8 to 10 minutes or until golden brown. Mix together margarine and garlic powder; brush over tops of biscuits. Serve warm.

Buttermilk Biscuits

2¼ cups flour

1 cup buttermilk

¼ cup oil

Preheat oven to 450°. Mix together flour, milk and oil. Flour your hands and roll dough into 8 round medium-sized balls. Pat into a 9-inch greased round pan. Bake 12 to 15 minutes or until tops are browned.

My favorite Buttermilk Biscuits are delicious with tomato or sausage gravy. Some people, like my daddy for example, enjoy them served with butter and syrup. To me, it's great either way.

Sausage Gravy

1 pound pork sausage

3 tablespoons flour

1 pint half and half

Hot buttermilk biscuits

Brown sausage. Remove sausage to a bowl, reserving drippings in skillet. Stir flour into drippings. Pour in ½ of the half and half. Stir; simmer until starts to thicken. Stir in sausage and remaining half and half. Continue to simmer until gravy is thick. Serve over hot buttermilk biscuits.

Grandma's Tomato Gravy

4 tablespoons oil

2 or 3 tablespoons flour

Salt and pepper

1 (15-ounce) can diced tomatoes, drained

1 cup water

1 (8-ounce) can tomato sauce

Heat oil in a large skillet over medium heat; stir in flour. Cook and stir until light brown. Season to taste with salt and pepper. Pour in diced tomatoes and 1 cup water; stir well. Reduce heat. Pour in tomato sauce. Stir. Cover and simmer 15 minutes or until thick.

My grandma, "Marene" (Mah-reen-ee) always made me Tomato Gravy. Even though she is not with us now, I am reminded of her every time we have tomato gravy.

Sweet Cornbread Muffins

2 large eggs

1 cup milk

¼ cup vegetable oil

1½ cups plain yellow cornmeal

1 cup self-rising flour

¼ cup sugar

¾ teaspoon salt

Preheat oven to 450°. Combine all ingredients and mix well until mixture is creamy and smooth. Pour evenly into muffin pans. Bake approximately 20 to 25 minutes or until lightly browned on top.

istockphoto / mcFields

Melt in Your Mouth Rolls

2 sticks butter, softened

2 cups self-rising flour

1 (8-ounce) carton sour cream

Preheat oven to 400°. Mix all ingredients. Drop by tablespoon in greased mini-muffin pan. Bake 10 to 12 minutes or until brown.

Spoon Rolls

1 package yeast

2 cups hot water

¾ cup butter Crisco, melted

¼ cup sugar

1 egg

4 cups self-rising flour

Mix together yeast with hot water. In a separate bowl; mix Crisco with sugar, egg, and flour. Add in yeast and water. Mix well; spoon into greased muffin pans. Bake 20 minutes at 350°.

Hot Buns? We all love them. To keep your rolls warmer longer, put a sheet of tin foil, under the napkin in your bread basket.

Try these Spoon Rolls hot out of the oven with honey butter so the butter just rolls off the top. Yum!

Easy Caramel Rolls

2 loaves frozen white bread dough

1 small package butterscotch pudding (not instant)

2 tablespoons milk

1 cup brown sugar

½ cup butter, melted

1 teaspoon cinnamon

Partially thaw bread and cut into small chunks. Place in a greased 9x13-inch pan. Mix together remaining ingredients and pour over bread slices. Let rise 1½ hours. Bake 350° for 30 minutes.

Bread

Sweet Cinnamon Rolls

2 cups sifted all-purpose flour

1 tablespoon plus 1 teaspoon baking powder

1 teaspoon salt

¼ teaspoon baking soda

¼ cup vegetable oil

¾ cup buttermilk

1 stick butter, softened

¾ cup sugar

1 teaspoon cinnamon

1 cup milk, optional

Combine flour, baking powder, salt and baking soda in a medium bowl and mix well. Stir in vegetable oil. Add buttermilk and stir until blended. Knead dough on a lightly floured surface until smooth. Roll dough into a 8x15-inch rectangle. Preheat oven at 400°. Grease a 9-inch round baking pan lightly. Spread butter over dough. Combine sugar and cinnamon in a small bowl and mix well. Sprinkle over butter. Roll up rectangle, jelly-roll fashion, starting from long side. Pinch seam to seal. Cut roll into 1½-inch slices. Place in prepared pan. Bake 15 to 20 minutes or until lightly browned. Pour milk over top, if desired. Serve hot.

Cream Cheese Danish

2 packages crescent rolls, divided

2 (8-ounce) packages cream cheese, softened

1 cup sugar

1 egg, separated

1 teaspoon vanilla

3 tablespoons milk

1 cup powdered sugar

Unroll 1 package crescent rolls and place in bottom of greased 9x13-inch baking pan. Combine cream cheese, sugar, egg yolk, and vanilla. Spread over rolls in pan. Layer remaining package crescent rolls over that. Beat egg white with a fork and brush on top. Bake 350° for 30 minutes.

Icing

1 cup powdered sugar

3 tablespoons milk

Mix well and pour over Danish.

Coffee with your pastry? When your coffee grinder needs a good cleaning, use rice. Place a small amount in the grinder and run it as normal. When you dump the rice, the grinder is clean.

Good Morning Coffee Cake

1 yellow cake mix

1 (3.4-ounce) box instant vanilla pudding mix

1 (8-ounce) carton sour cream

4 eggs, beaten

⅓ cup canola oil

2 teaspoons vanilla extract

⅔ cup chopped pecans

⅓ cup sugar

2 teaspoons ground cinnamon

½ cup powdered sugar

2 tablespoons orange juice (or water if preferred)

In a large bowl, combine dry cake mix, dry pudding mix, sour cream, eggs, oil and vanilla. Beat with an electric mixer until fully mixed. Pour into a greased 9x13-inch pan. In a small bowl, combine pecans, sugar and cinnamon; sprinkle over batter. Use a butter knife to swirl pecan mixture throughout batter. Bake at 350° for 30 to 35 minutes or until a toothpick inserted in the center comes out clean. While cake is baking, combine powdered sugar and orange juice until smooth; drizzle over warm coffee cake.

Monkey Bread

1¾ cups sugar, divided

1 tablespoon cinnamon

4 cans biscuits

1½ sticks butter, melted

Mix ¾ cups sugar and cinnamon together. Cut each biscuit into 4 pieces and roll each into a ball. Roll into sugar mixture. Put into a greased Bundt pan. Mix remaining 1 cup sugar with melted butter and pour over biscuits. Bake at 425° for 40 minutes.

Nut Bread

1 pound brown sugar

4 eggs

2 teaspoons vanilla

2 cups flour

2 cups chopped pecans

Beat sugar and eggs with an electric mixer on low until smooth. Add vanilla and flour and continue to beat until well mixed. Gently stir in pecans. Pour into a greased 8-inch square baking dish. Bake at 350° for 40 to 45 minutes or until a toothpick inserted in the center comes out clean.

bigstockphoto / mcfields

Christmas Bread

1 cup shortening

1 cup sugar

2 eggs

2 cups flour

¼ teaspoon salt

1 teaspoon baking soda

3 bananas, mashed

1 cup chopped nuts

¼ cup chocolate chips

¼ cup maraschino cherries

Cream shortening with sugar until smooth; add eggs one at a time, mixing well after each addition. Combine flour, salt and baking soda. Stir into creamed mixture. Stir in bananas and mix well. Stir in nuts, chips and cherries. Divide and bake in 2 separate, treated small loaf pans. Bake at 350° for 1 hour.

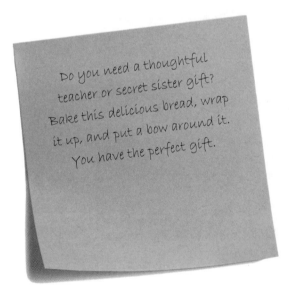

Do you need a thoughtful teacher or secret sister gift? Bake this delicious bread, wrap it up, and put a bow around it. You have the perfect gift.

Butter Bread

1 butter pecan cake mix

1 small box instant coconut pudding mix

½ cup oil

4 eggs

1 cup hot water

1 teaspoon vanilla

Mix all together. Pour into a greased loaf pan. Bake 350° for 15 minutes. Reduce heat to 300° and bake 30 to 40 minutes.

Poppy Seed Bread

3 cups flour

1½ teaspoons salt

1½ teaspoons baking powder

1½ cups milk

2½ cups sugar

1⅛ cups oil

1½ teaspoons poppy seeds

3 eggs

1½ teaspoons vanilla

1½ teaspoons almond extract

Mix all ingredients together; beat 2 minutes. Grease and flour 2 loaf pans; pour mixture into pans and bake at 350° for 1 hour and 15 minutes.

Glaze

¾ cup sugar

½ teaspoon almond extract

¼ cup orange juice

½ teaspoon vanilla

Mix all ingredients together and spread over warm bread.

Amish White Bread

2 cups warm water

⅔ cup sugar

1½ tablespoons active dry yeast

1½ teaspoons salt

¼ cup vegetable oil

6 cups bread flour

Bread

In a large bowl, dissolve sugar in warm water; stir in yeast. Allow to proof until yeast resembles creamy foam. Mix salt and oil into yeast. Mix in flour, 1 cup at a time. Knead dough on a lightly floured surface until smooth. Place in a well-oiled bowl, and turn dough to coat. Cover with a damp cloth. Allow to rise 1 hour. Punch dough down, knead for a few minutes. Divide in half. Shape into loaves, and place into 2 treated 9x5-inch loaf pans. Allow to rise 30 minutes. Bake at 350° for 30 minutes.

Sesame Onion Twists

2 tablespoons butter

1½ cups finely chopped onions

¼ teaspoon paprika

1 (16-ounce) loaf frozen bread dough, thawed

1 large egg, beaten

1 tablespoon sesame seeds

Melt butter in medium skillet. Add chopped onion and paprika; cook until onion is tender, stirring constantly. Remove from heat. Roll thawed dough into a 12x14-inch rectangle. Spread onion mixture on one side of dough. Fold dough over onion mixture to make a 6x14-inch rectangle. Pinch edges together to seal over onion mixture. Cut dough into 12 lengthwise dough strips. Gently twist 1 dough strip 2 times and place on prepared buttered baking sheet. Press down both ends of dough strip to prevent curling. Repeat with remaining dough strips. Cover twists with a towel, and let rise 40 minutes in a warm area. Brush with beaten egg; sprinkle with sesame seeds. Bake at 375° until golden brown, about 15 to 18 minutes.

Mrs. Vicki's Mexican Cornbread

1 cup buttermilk

2 eggs

⅓ cup oil

1½ cups self-rising cornmeal

¼ cup finely chopped jalapeño peppers

½ cup chopped onions

1 cup shredded Cheddar cheese

1 cup cream corn

¼ teaspoon baking powder, optional

Preheat oven to 425°. Place a greased cast-iron skillet in oven to get hot while preheating. Mix all ingredients and pour into heated skillet. Bake until top of cornbread is golden brown.

Every chance I get, I ask Mrs. Vicki to make HER Mexican Cornbread. No one makes it like her. I love it so much, she will randomly make a pan and bring it to the house just for me.

Nobody enjoys rubbery reheated bread from the microwave. Your family deserves better, so next time try this trick. Place a cup of water in the microwave with your sliced bread, biscuits, pancakes or muffins, and reheat. The water will keep them moist and help them reheat faster.

Oyster Dressing

1 medium onion, chopped

2 stalks celery, chopped

¼ stick butter

1 (1-pound) package dried breadcrumbs

Salt and pepper to taste

1 egg, beaten

½ cup chicken stock, heated

½ pint oysters, drained and rinsed

Sauté onion and celery in butter. Combine breadcrumbs, seasoning and egg. Add chicken stock and onion mixture to breadcrumbs mix. Add oysters and mix well. Bake at 350° for 45 minutes to 1 hour until golden brown.

The End. Is your family like mine? No one ever eats the end pieces of the bread. We end up feeding them to the birds or throwing them away. Here's an idea. Save those end pieces in a ziplock bag in the freezer. When your bag is full, run the bread through the blender or food chopper to make your own breadcrumbs.

Next time you make dressing, definitely try Mrs. Vicki's 3-Day Dressing, you will never find a better recipe.

Mrs. Vicki's 3-Day Cornbread Dressing

Day 1, Cornbread

4 cups Martha White self-rising yellow cornmeal

1 medium onion and 1 celery stalk, chopped fine

4 eggs

1 to 1½ cups buttermilk

1 stick butter, melted

Preheat oven to 400°. Combine all ingredients; mix well. Bake in 2 large greased baking pans about 30 minutes or until brown. Cool then crumble into a large bowl with lid. Seal tight and refrigerate 24 hours to blend flavors.

Day 2, Dressing

8 to 10 cups water

4 chicken breasts, skins on

1 small onion and 2 stalks celery, chopped fine

Seasoned salt, black pepper, onion powder

Crumbled cornbread

2 boxes Stove Top Chicken-Flavor Dressing Mix

1 stick butter, melted

1 (26-ounce) can Campbell's cream of chicken soup

2 (10¾-ounce) cans cream of celery soup

In a large boiler, bring chicken breast, onion, celery and seasonings to a boil. Boil until chicken is tender and white. Reserve chicken for another use. Using clean hands, mix together crumbled cornbread and Stove Top Dressing. Mix well. Stir in melted butter and soups. Mix well. Slowly add broth, 1 cup at a time, resting about 2 minutes between each cup. Mix well. Mixture should not be soupy but not too dry. Cool to room temperature. Refrigerate overnight. Refrigerate remaining broth for next day.

Day 3, Cook & Serve

Dressing mixture from refrigerator

4 eggs, beaten

1 stick butter, divided

Remove dressing mixture from refrigerator. Let stand on counter 30 minutes to reach room temperature. Stir in eggs. Mix well. If consistency seems too dry, add a small amount of reserved chicken broth. Melt ½ stick butter in each of 2 large baking pans. Spray sides of pan with non-stick cooking spray. Divide dressing evenly between 2 pans. Bake at 400° about 45 minutes or until set in middle.

Mary's Potato Soup

4 cups peeled and cubed potatoes

1 cup diced celery

1 cup coarsely chopped onion

2 teaspoons salt

2 cups water

1 cup milk

1 cup whipping cream

3 tablespoons melted butter

1 tablespoon dried parsley flakes

⅛ teaspoon pepper

Cook potatoes, celery, onion and salt in water 20 minutes or until potatoes are tender. Stir in remaining ingredients. Lightly mash with a potato masher and cook stirring constantly until soup is hot and thickened.

istockphoto / Christine Glade

Tony's Potato Soup

2½ to 3 pounds potatoes, peeled and cubed

1 (8-ounce) package Philadelphia cream cheese with chives

Dash milk

1 package bacon, fried crisp and crumbled

½ cup flour, sifted

½ teaspoon butter

Salt and pepper

1 onion diced, optional

In a large boiler, cover potatoes with water. Boil until slightly tender. Drain off ½ water. Stir in remaining ingredients. Simmer over medium-low heat until cooked down to desired consistency, about 1 hour. Serve with cornbread.

The weather outside might be frightful, but any winter day is a good day for potato soup. Tony's Potato Soup is a good, thick and hearty soup. Try Mary's Potato Soup with shredded cheese on top. Both are delicious with a slice of hot cornbread on the side.

Broccoli Soup

1 pound frozen chopped broccoli

1 pound Velveeta cheese, cubed

1 (10¾-ounce) can cream of celery soup

1 (14½-ounce) can chicken broth

Salt and pepper to taste

Combine all ingredients in a crockpot. Cover. Cook on low 5 to 6 hours.

Chicken Noodle Soup

1 pound chicken, cubed

2 medium onions, chopped

½ stick butter

1 can cream of chicken soup

1 can cream of celery soup

2 chicken bouillon cubes

Salt and pepper

1 bag wide egg noodles

Sauté chicken and onions in butter in a large pot. Add water to almost full. Add soups and cook over medium heat, stirring occasionally, until chicken is done. Add chicken bouillon, and season to taste with salt and pepper. Add egg noodles; cook 5 minutes. Cover and simmer 15 minutes. Enjoy with crackers.

When my kids are sick, I make them Chicken Noodle Soup. This is the recipe my Granny Bobbie made when I was sick. It's good and easy.

Just Good Soup

2 envelopes brown gravy mix

2 cups cold water

1 onion, chopped

2 chicken breasts, chopped

2 cups chopped deer tenderloin

1 can golden cream of mushroom soup

¼ cup Frank's hot sauce

Salt and pepper to taste

Onion powder and garlic powder to taste

Combine all ingredients in a large crockpot. Cook on high 6 hours. Reduce heat to low and cook additional 2 hours.

Quicker than Quick Chicken Taco Soup

1 (14-ounce) can chicken broth

1 (16-ounce) jar mild thick and chunky salsa

1 (15-ounce) can ranch-style beans

1 (15-ounce) can whole-kernel corn

1 (12-ounce) can chicken breast

In a medium stew pot, combine all ingredients. Cover and cook over medium for 20 minutes. Reduce heat to low. Simmer 10 minutes. Remove from heat and serve.

Taco Soup

2 pounds lean hamburger meat

1 package taco seasoning mix

2 cans whole-kernel corn, drained

2 cans red beans, drained

2 cans stewed tomatoes, drained

1 pound cubed Velveeta cheese

Fritos brand corn chips

Sour cream, optional

Brown meat; drain. Add taco seasoning to meat with 3 tablespoons water. Simmer. Add vegetables and cheese. Simmer over low heat until cheese melts. Serve over Fritos and topped with sour cream.

Chili Soup

1 pound ground beef

2 (16-ounce) cans pinto beans, drained

2 cans Mexican corn, drained

1 medium onion, chopped

1 can diced tomatoes

2 envelopes McCormick's taco seasoning

1 large can V8 tomato soup

1 can mild Ro-Tel

2 tablespoons chili powder

Brown hamburger meat; drain. In a large boiler, combine all ingredients. Simmer 1 hour. Serve to your family with hot cornbread during the first cold snap of the year.

Stew for a Crowd

2 chickens

3 pounds hamburger meat

1 (5-pound) bag potatoes, peeled and chopped

3 quarts tomatoes

3 large onions, chopped

3 cans cream-style corn

Salt and pepper to taste

Chili powder to taste

¼ cup sugar

Boil chicken in a large stockpot; debone chicken reserving broth in pot. Brown hamburger; drain. Return chicken to broth with browned hamburger, potatoes, tomatoes and onions. Cook over low heat until about 20 minutes before you are ready serve, at least 1 hour. Mix in corn, salt, pepper and chili powder. Add ¼ cup sugar; stir. Continue to cook on low for 20 minutes.

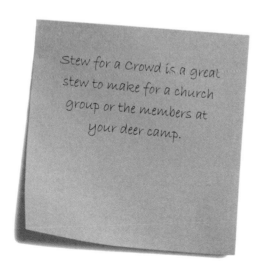

Stew for a Crowd is a great stew to make for a church group or the members at your deer camp.

Beef & Sausage Stew

3 pounds beef stew meat

½ cup plus 2 tablespoons all-purpose flour, divided

1 (16-ounce) can diced tomatoes, with juice

½ pound smoked sausage, sliced

3 potatoes, peeled and diced

1 cup chopped leeks

1 cup chopped onions

4 celery stalks, sliced

½ cup chicken broth

3 cloves garlic, minced

3 tablespoons water

Trim fat from beef; cut beef into ¾-inch cubes. Set aside. Place ½ cup flour in resealable plastic bag. Add beef; seal bag. Shake bag to coat beef cubes with flour. Place beef cubes in slow cooker. Add tomatoes with juice, sausage, potatoes, leeks, onions, celery, chicken broth and garlic. Stir well. Cover slow cooker and cook on high 4 to 6 hours. Combine remaining 2 tablespoons flour with 3 tablespoons water into a small bowl; stir until mixture becomes a paste. Stir flour mixture into slow cooker; mix well. Cover and cook until thickened, about 10 to 15 minutes. Serve with buttermilk biscuits or in a bread bowl.

Crockpot Beef Stew

2 pounds beef stew meat

½ cup all-purpose flour

3 tablespoons shortening

1 medium onion, chopped

4 carrots, sliced

3 celery stalks, sliced

1 clove garlic, minced

2 bay leaves

1 teaspoon each salt and sugar

½ teaspoon each pepper and paprika

1 teaspoon lemon juice

1 teaspoon Worcestershire sauce

4 cups water

Dredge meat in flour. Melt shortening in skillet. Slightly brown both sides of beef cubes in shortening. Remove to crockpot and add remaining ingredients; stir. Cover and cook on high 5 to 6 hours. Serve over rice.

Don't peek! I know it's hard, but resist opening the lid when cooking in your slow cooker crockpot. The steam that condenses on the lid helps cook food from the top. Even a quick peek means the cooker loses its steam increasing the cook time. It can take up to 20 minutes for your crockpot to regain the lost steam and temperature.

Down Home Crockpot Stew

Soups

1 pound deer burger

1 onion, diced

5 medium potatoes, washed and peeled

1 (14.5-ounce) can string beans

1 (14.5-ounce) can red kidney beans

1½ cups frozen fresh yellow cut corn

2 (12-ounce) cans V8 Vegetable Juice

1 (14.5-ounce) can tomato sauce

¼ cup hot sauce

Pepper, garlic powder and onion powder, to taste

In a medium skillet, brown deer burger with onions; drain. Dice potatoes. Combine all ingredients into a large crockpot. Cook on high 5 hours, stirring occasionally. Serve with cornbread.

Iris Savell's Shrimp Etouffee

2 bundles green onions with stems, chopped

¼ cup parsley flakes

Vegetable oil

2 (64-ounce) cans V8 Cocktail Juice

1 (10-ounce) can mild Ro-Tel

2 cans cream of mushroom soup

1 to 2 pounds large shrimp, peeled and deveined

Flour

In a large gumbo pot, sauté onions and parsley in small amount of oil; drain. Combine sautéed onions, cocktail juice, Ro-Tel, and mushroom soup; bring to a boil. Reduce heat and simmer 45 minutes. Shake shrimp in flour until fully covered. Pour into pot. Stir well. Cook 8 minutes. Serve over rice.

Chicken & Sausage Gumbo

1 cup chopped onion

½ cup chopped bell pepper

½ pound smoked sausage

¾ cup all-purpose flour

¾ pound chicken breasts, cooked and shredded

¾ cup chopped green onions

½ cup chopped celery

8 cups water

2 cloves garlic, chopped

1 bay leaf

1½ teaspoons Cajun seasoning

1 teaspoon salt

½ teaspoon dried thyme

¼ teaspoon black pepper

1 tablespoon Worcestershire

Dash hot sauce

4 cups cooked rice

Sauté onions, bell pepper and sausage in a large skillet. Drain fat. In a large crockpot, combine all ingredients. Cook on high 3 to 4 hours.

thinkstock / istockphoto / sf_foodphoto

Broccoli Salad

2 bunches fresh broccoli

1 small onion, chopped

1 pound bacon, cooked and crumbled

¼ cup chopped pecans

1 cup mayonnaise

½ cup sugar

1 tablespoon apple cider vinegar

Cut broccoli crowns from stalks; discard stalks. Mix onion, bacon, pecans, mayonnaise, sugar and vinegar. Stir well. Pour dressing over broccoli crowns just before serving.

My kids often do not like the strong taste of raw onion. So, I soak the diced or sliced raw onions in ice water about 15 minutes before adding them to salads. It mellows the taste and the smell.

Beet & Pickle Salad

2 cans beets, sliced and drained

8 baby dill pickles, sliced

½ cup thinly sliced red or Spanish onion

2 tablespoons fresh dill

¼ cup red wine vinegar

3 tablespoons vegetable oil

1 tablespoon sugar

1 teaspoon Dijon mustard

1 teaspoon prepared horseradish, optional

Combine beets, pickles, onions, and dill in a medium bowl. In a small saucepan, stir together remaining ingredients. Heat, stirring constantly, until almost boiling. Cool to lukewarm. Pour dressing over salad and toss to coat. Chill at least 1 hour.

Cornbread Salad

1 pan prepared and cooked cornbread, cooled

1 envelope dry ranch dressing mix

1 cup sour cream

1 cup mayonnaise

2 to 3 tomatoes, chopped

½ cup chopped red bell pepper

½ cup chopped green bell pepper

½ cup chopped green onions

½ cup cauliflower

½ cup broccoli

2 (16-ounce) cans pinto beans

2 cups shredded Cheddar cheese

10 slices bacon, fried very crisp and crumbled

2 cans whole-kernel corn, well drained

Crumble ½ cornbread in a large bowl; set aside. Stir together salad dressing mix, sour cream and mayonnaise; until well blended set aside. Combine tomatoes, bell peppers, onions, cauliflower and broccoli. Toss gently. Layer 1 can beans, ½ tomato mixture, 1 cup cheese, ½ bacon and 1 can corn. Top with ½ dressing. Repeat layers. Cover and chill at least 5 hours. Stir to mix everything together just before serving.

istockphoto / Imagesbybarbara

Greek-Style Pasta Salad

1 (12-ounce) box tri-colored pasta

1 (3.8-ounce) can sliced black olives

¼ cup grated Parmesan cheese

½ cup sliced cherry tomatoes

Cook pasta according to directions on box; drain.
Stir in all other ingredients.

Dressing

4 tablespoons mayonnaise

¾ cup olive oil

4 tablespoons lemon juice

4 tablespoons Cavender's Greek seasoning

Mix dressing ingredients all together and toss with
pasta. Refrigerate at least 12 hours before serving.

Easy Shrimp Salad

1 (8-ounce) package elbow macaroni

1 small jar chopped pimentos

1 cup chopped dill pickles

1 cup chopped celery

½ cup finely chopped onions

1 small can chopped baby shrimp, drained

4 hard-boiled eggs, chopped

1 cup mayonnaise

Salt and pepper to taste

Boil macaroni as directed; drain. Stir in pimentos, pickles, celery, onion,
shrimp and eggs. Stir in mayonnaise to your liking. Salt and pepper to taste.

Macaroni Salad

1 (7-ounce) box elbow macaroni, cooked and drained

2 ribs celery, minced fine

1 tablespoon dry minced onion

⅓ cup diced sweet pickles

1½ cups Miracle Whip

½ cup Kraft mayonnaise

¼ teaspoon black pepper

¼ teaspoon dry mustard

1 teaspoon sugar

Salt to taste

Combine everything just as listed. Refrigerate in a tightly covered dish several hours before serving.

Ham & Crab Salad

6 slices ham, chopped fine

1 small tomato, chopped

2 whole dill pickles, chopped fine

1 cup chopped crabmeat

3 to 4 tablespoons mayonnaise

¼ cup ranch dressing

¼ cup real bacon pieces

Salt and pepper

Mix all ingredients. Serve on white bread or enjoy with crackers.

Taco Salad

5 pounds ground chuck

3 packages taco seasoning

1 package spicy chili seasoning

1 (10-ounce) can diced tomatoes with green chiles

1 medium onion, chopped finely

6 medium fresh jalapeno peppers, chopped

1 (1-pound) bag salad greens

1 to 2 (8-ounce) bags finely shredded cheese

1 (8-ounce) tub sour cream

1 (16-ounce) bag restaurant-style tortilla chips

Brown ground chuck; drain and reserve liquid. Add seasoning packets to meat, adding back liquid (or water, if you prefer) as needed to maintain moist consistency. Make all other ingredients individually available buffet-style.

Salads

Everyone's Favorite Potato Salad

4 pounds potatoes, peeled and cubed

½ to 1 cup mayonnaise

¼ cup mustard

2½ tablespoons dill pickle relish

3 hard boiled eggs, chopped

Salt and pepper to taste

2 tablespoons milk

2 tablespoons butter

Boil potatoes until tender; drain. Beat potatoes with a mixer until smooth. Stir in milk, butter, mayonnaise, pickle relish, eggs, mustard, salt and pepper. Stir well. Serve cold.

When visiting my Papaw Victor, I always make him a big bowl of potato salad. He loves it! I enjoy seeing his smile when he knows I made this just for him. My husband loves it too, and will eat only my potato salad.

Holiday Chicken Salad

1 cup mayonnaise

1 teaspoon paprika

1 teaspoon season salt

1½ cups dried apples

1 cup chopped celery

Pepper

½ cup bell pepper

2 green onions, chopped

1 cup chopped pecans

4 cups cubed cooked chicken

Mix all ingredients together well. Chill before serving.

bigstockphoto / Chas53

Mississippi Kumback Sauce

2 cloves garlic, minced

¼ cup chili sauce

¼ cup ketchup

1 tablespoon Worcestershire sauce

1 dash Tabasco

1 tablespoon grated onion

½ tablespoon vinegar

1 cup mayonnaise

1 tablespoon prepared mustard

½ cup salad oil

½ teaspoon black pepper

Dash paprika

2 tablespoons water

Combine all ingredients in a jar; seal. Shake well. Keep refrigerated until ready to use.

Kumback Sauce is a favorite in Mississippi. It's called Kumback Sauce because once you have it, you definitely will come back for more. It makes a great salad dressing, and is also good on sandwiches or as a veggie dip.

Cherry Salad

1 can cherry pie filling

1 box cherry Jell-O

1 small can crushed pineapple

1 cup chopped pecans

Bring cherries to a boil; add Jell-O. Remove from heat. Add pineapple and chopped pecans. Refrigerate in a pretty bowl or serving dish. Serve when set or next day.

Pistachio Salad

1 box pistachio pudding mix

1 (8-ounce) carton whipped topping

1 cup mini marshmallows

1 cup chopped pecans

1 small can crushed pineapple, drained

Mix all and chill.

FLOUR

Six Cup Salad

1 cup sour cream

1 cup chopped pecans

1 cup fruit cocktail, drained

1 cup mandarin oranges, drained

1 cup pineapple chunks, drained

1 cup mini marshmallows

Mix all; chill before serving.

Iris's Lime Jell-O Salad

5 (8-ounce) cartons whipped topping

8 small boxes sugar-free lime Jell-O

1 large carton cottage cheese

1 large can crushed pineapple

Pecans, chopped

Combine whipped topping and dry lime Jell-O mix. Stir in cottage cheese, crushed pineapple, and pecans. Mix well. Chill in refrigerator before serving.

bigstockphoto / Brebra

Las Vegas Fruit Salad

1 (6-ounce) can frozen orange juice

1 large box instant vanilla pudding

1 large carton whipped topping

1 (8-ounce) carton sour cream

1 large can sliced peaches, drained

1 large can pineapple tidbits, drained

1 cup chopped apples

½ cup chopped pecans

2 bananas, sliced

With a mixer; mix orange juice, pudding and whipped topping. Mix in sour cream and blend. Mix in remaining fruit and blend well.

To prolong the life of cottage cheese, turn the carton upside down in the refrigerator once opened.

Las Vegas Fruit Salad is good served alone or over pound cake.

Won't Be Any Left Black-Eyed Peas

1 large bag frozen black-eyed peas

2 packs Goya ham seasoning

Salt and pepper

2 teaspoons celery salt

1 teaspoon garlic powder

1 teaspoon onion powder

1 teaspoon garlic and pepper seasoning

Pour peas in a large boiler. Cover with water. Bring to a boil. Let boil about 15 minutes. Stir in ham seasoning and remaining seasonings. Reduce heat. Add more water if needed. Slowly boil additional 20 to 25 minutes or until peas are tender. Serve over fresh cornbread.

Serving Cornbread? These black-eyed peas are a must. They are loaded with flavor, and even better if you mix a little mayonnaise in once your plate is fixed. Or, tempt your taste buds with a little Frank's hot sauce on top.... mmmm good!

Chuck Wagon Beans

1 (1-pound) can kidney beans, drained

1 (1-pound) can butter beans, drained

1 cup barbecue sauce

1 (3½-ounce) can French fried onions

4 slices bacon, diced

In a 9x13-inch casserole pan, combine beans, barbecue sauce, and French fried onions. Place bacon on top. Bake at 350° for 45 minutes.

Krista's Baked Beans

1 pound ground hamburger meat

½ small onion, chopped

1 (15-ounce) can crushed pineapple, drained

¼ cup light brown sugar

1 (16-ounce) can KC Masterpiece Smoky Bourbon Baked Beans

1 (28-ounce) can Bush's Maple Cured Bacon Baked Beans

¼ cup honey barbecue sauce

Salt and pepper to taste

Garlic powder to taste

In a medium skillet, brown hamburger meat with onion. Drain. In a treated large crockpot, add pineapple and brown sugar. Stir well. Stir in beans, meat and barbecue sauce. Season to taste; stir well. Cook on high 1 hour or until hot and bubbly.

Green Bean Casserole

2 cans seasoned green beans, drained

1 can cream of mushroom soup

¼ cup milk

Dash pepper

1½ cups French fried onions, divided

½ cup shredded Cheddar cheese

Place green beans in greased casserole dish. Stir in soup, milk and pepper. Carefully stir in 1 cup French fried onions and cheese. Bake at 350° for 30 minutes. Top with remaining onions, bake additional 5 minutes.

My Green Bean Casserole is great served for Christmas, Thanksgiving or family reunions. Make plenty. It will be the first thing to go.

Aunt June's String Bean & Bacon Bundles are delish. Wrapping the beans can be a little time consuming, but the end result is worth the effort.

Aunt June's String Bean & Bacon Bundles

3 cans whole green beans

1 bottle Italian dressing

1½ packs bacon

Toothpicks

Drain and rinse green beans. Soak in Italian dressing overnight. Cut bacon in ½ strips. Roll up 8 beans at a time and secure with toothpick. Repeat until all green beans are used. Bake at 375° until bacon is crispy.

Spinach & Rice Casserole

1 package frozen spinach, cooked and drained

1 pound sharp Cheddar cheese, shredded

1 cup milk

4 eggs, beaten

1 tablespoon onion, finely chopped

1 tablespoon Worcestershire sauce

2 teaspoons salt

¼ teaspoon thyme

¼ teaspoon rosemary

¼ teaspoon marjoram

¼ cup melted butter

3 cups cooked rice

Mix all ingredients together. Bake in a 2-quart casserole dish set in a pan of hot water. Bake at 350° for 1 hour and 15 minutes.

Vegetable Casserole

2 (16-ounce) cans Veg-All, drained

2 cups shredded Cheddar cheese

1 cup chopped onions

¼ cup chopped celery, optional

1 cup mayonnaise

1 cup crushed Ritz crackers

1 stick margarine

Mix Veg-All, cheese, onions, celery and mayonnaise together. Place in 9x13-inch baking dish. Cover with Ritz crackers. Melt margarine and pour over crackers. Bake at 350° for 30 minutes.

Turnip Green Casserole

1 can chopped turnip greens, drained well

½ cup mayonnaise

½ can cream of mushroom soup

2 eggs, beaten

1½ tablespoons white vinegar

1 teaspoon horseradish

Salt and pepper to taste

Shredded Cheddar cheese, enough to cover top

Combine all ingredients, except cheese. Bake at 350° for 1 hour. During the last 5 minutes, sprinkle cheese on top.

Big B's Collard Greens

1 large ham hock

2 quarts chicken stock

1 large onion, minced

4 garlic cloves, minced

2 tablespoons crushed red pepper flakes

¼ teaspoon black pepper

1 large bunch collard greens, rinsed and chopped

3 tablespoons cider vinegar

Salt to taste

Hot sauce

Add ham hock to large pot; add chicken stock, onion, garlic, red pepper flakes and black pepper. Bring to a boil and reduce heat to a simmer; simmer 1 to 2 hours to make a rich broth. Add collard greens and vinegar; simmer 1 to 5 hours depending on texture you prefer. Salt to taste and serve in a bowl with hot sauce to add individually. These are super-good with a broth that comes out like soup.

Big B's Collard Greens are food for the soul. They are great over crumbled cornbread and washed down with a glass of milk. For a real treat, serve them with fresh fried catfish.

Baked Corn Casserole

1 can cream-style corn

1 can whole-kernel corn

1 large onion, chopped

1 medium bell pepper, chopped

1 (2-ounce) jar chopped pimento

⅔ cup milk

1 egg, well beaten

1 cup cracker crumbs

1 cup shredded cheese

¼ cup melted butter

Salt, pepper, and red pepper to taste

Combine all ingredients in order given and mix well. Pour into greased 2-quart casserole dish and bake at 350° for 1 hour.

Tastes Like Fried Corn

3 strips bacon

1 can white whole-kernel corn

1 can yellow cream-style corn

Fry bacon very crisp in skillet. Remove bacon. Pour both cans of corn into bacon grease. Crumble bacon strips and add to corn. Stir on low heat for 5 minutes.

Kristen's Easy Squash Casserole

1 pound yellow squash, cooked, drained and mashed

¼ cup butter, melted

2 cups shredded cheese plus more for topping

1 medium onion, chopped

1 egg, beaten

Salt and pepper to taste

1 roll Ritz crackers, crushed (divided)

Mix all ingredients, using only ½ crackers, and put in 1½-quart casserole. Sprinkle remaining cracker crumbs on top and bake at 400° for 30 minutes or until firm and slightly brown. Sprinkle additional cheese on top. Cover and return to oven just enough to melt cheese.

Squash & Water Chestnut Casserole

2 cups yellow squash, cooked and drained

1 can cream of mushroom soup

¼ pack saltines, crushed

½ stick margarine, melted

Black pepper to taste

½ cup thinly sliced water chestnuts

1 tablespoon minced onion flakes

Dash Worcestershire sauce

1 tablespoon chopped pimentos

Shredded Cheese

Combine all ingredients except shredded cheese. (If this mixture seems a little too thick, add a little milk.) Mix well. Pour into a buttered casserole dish. Bake at 350° for 20 minutes. Remove from oven, top with cheese, and return just long enough to melt cheese.

Southern Fried Okra

1 pound fresh okra

Salt and pepper

¾ cup buttermilk

1 cup flour

1 teaspoon baking powder

Oil for frying

Slice okra in ½-inch pieces; salt and pepper to taste. Pour into flat bottomed bowl and toss with buttermilk. Let stand 30 minutes. Mix flour with baking powder and season with salt and pepper. Remove okra from buttermilk into flour mixture and coat well. Fry in hot oil until brown.

My mother-in-law, Mrs. Vicki, says this is the only way to make fried okra. I like it with a few shakes of hot sauce over the top.

Creole Okra

2 cups sliced okra

2 tablespoons minced onion

2 tablespoons minced green bell pepper

1 tablespoon margarine

2 cups chopped tomatoes

2 teaspoons sugar

½ teaspoon salt

¼ teaspoon pepper

Sauté okra, onion and pepper in margarine 5 minutes; stirring constantly. Stir in remaining ingredients. Cook over low heat 10 to 15 minutes; stirring occasionally. Serve.

bigstockphoto / Rohit Seth

Fried Green Tomatoes

3 green tomatoes, sliced ⅓-inch thick

½ cup buttermilk

2 eggs, slightly beaten

2 cups cornmeal

Salt and pepper to taste

Onion powder, optional

Garlic powder, optional

Oil for frying

In a large bowl, mix buttermilk and eggs together. Add tomatoes and soak at least 20 minutes. Combine cornmeal and seasoning in a large bowl. Batter tomatoes with cornmeal. Fry in hot oil until golden brown on both sides. Drain on a paper towel.

Green Tomato Casserole

6 medium green tomatoes, sliced in rounds

Salt and pepper to taste

1 cup Ritz cracker crumbs, divided

1 cup shredded sharp Cheddar cheese, divided

6 tablespoons butter, divided

Layer half tomatoes in a greased shallow dish. Sprinkle with salt and pepper. Add ½ cup cracker crumbs and ½ cup cheese. Dot with 3 tablespoons butter. Bake, covered at 350° for 30 minutes. Uncover, and bake 10 minutes or until brown.

Broccoli Casserole

1 package frozen broccoli

¾ cup rice

1 medium onion, chopped fine

1 stick butter

½ small jar Cheez Whiz

1 small can cream of mushroom soup

Salt and pepper to taste

Cook broccoli as directed on package; drain. Cook rice as directed on package. Sauté onions in butter. Combine broccoli, rice, onion and remaining ingredients in greased casserole dish. Bake at 350° for 30 minutes.

So Good Broccoli & Corn

⅓ cup oil

¼ cup finely chopped onion

3 cups frozen corn

3 cups frozen cut broccoli

3 tablespoons minced garlic

2 tablespoons lemon pepper

1 teaspoon salt

5 teaspoons Worcestershire sauce

Heat oil in a large skillet. Stir in remaining ingredients in order above. Reduce heat to medium. Stir and cover. Simmer 15 minutes stirring occasionally.

Honey Mustard Asparagus

1 (15-ounce) can asparagus spears

¼ cup plus 2 tablespoons honey

3 tablespoons Dijon mustard

3 tablespoons lemon juice

1 tablespoon plus 1 teaspoon olive oil

Prepare asparagus spears according to directions on label; drain. Mix honey, mustard, lemon juice and olive oil. Pour over asparagus. Serve.

Brown Sugar Asparagus

2 pounds asparagus spears

3 tablespoons butter

2 tablespoons light brown sugar

¾ cup chicken broth

Break off woody ends of asparagus; discard. Heat butter in a large skillet over medium heat. Stir in brown sugar and stir until sugar dissolves. Add asparagus to the brown sugar and sauté 2 minutes. Add chicken broth; bring to a boil. Reduce heat. Simmer 8 to 10 minutes. Remove asparagus from skillet, reserve juices. Continue to cook juices over medium heat, stirring frequently, until cooked down some. Pour over asparagus.

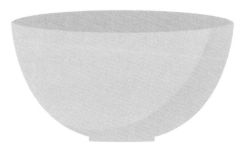

Carrot Casserole

1 onion, minced

1 cup finely chopped celery

3 tablespoons butter

3 cups cooked mashed carrots

2 eggs, slightly beaten

½ cup milk

1 teaspoon salt

½ cup breadcrumbs

In a skillet, sauté onion and celery in butter. Stir in mashed carrots. Add remaining ingredients and mix well. Pour into a buttered casserole dish and bake at 350° for 20 to 30 minutes.

Sweet Potato Casserole

3 cups mashed sweet potatoes

3 eggs

1 cup sugar

1 teaspoon vanilla flavoring

2 sticks margarine, melted (divided)

1 cup coconut

1 cup brown sugar

⅓ cup flour

1 cup chopped pecans

Mix potatoes, eggs, sugar, vanilla and 1 stick melted margarine and pour into a greased casserole dish. Mix coconut, brown sugar, flour and nuts with 1 stick melted margarine; spread over top of casserole. Bake 350° for 35 minutes.

Cabbage Au Gratin

1 medium head cabbage, chopped

⅓ cup vegetable oil

⅓ cup all-purpose flour

1 teaspoon salt

½ teaspoon pepper

1¾ cups milk

1 (8-ounce) package (2 cups) shredded Cheddar cheese

1½ cups breadcrumbs

4 tablespoons butter, melted

Place cabbage in a treated 4-quart casserole; set aside. In a saucepan, heat oil over medium heat. Stir in flour, salt and pepper; cook until bubbly. Gradually stir in milk; cook and stir until thickened. Fold in cheese. Pour over cabbage. Combine breadcrumbs and butter; sprinkle on top. Bake, uncovered, at 350° for 30 to 40 minutes or until bubbly.

Cabbage & Carrots

1 medium onion, chopped

2 tablespoons butter

4 medium carrots, thinly sliced

1 small head cabbage, chopped (about 6 cups)

½ cup chicken broth

1 teaspoon salt

1 teaspoon sugar

In a large skillet, saute onion in butter until tender. Add carrots; cook and stir 3 minutes. Stir in remaining ingredients; bring to a boil. Reduce heat. Cover and simmer about minutes or until vegetables are tender. Serve with a slotted spoon.

Steamed Cabbage

1 medium cabbage, shredded fine

1 teaspoon salt

¼ teaspoon black pepper

1 teaspoon sugar

½ stick margarine

7 tablespoons water

Combine all ingredients and steam 7 minutes.

When cooking cabbage place a small tin cup (or a can) half full of vinegar on the stove near the cabbage. It will absorb the odor.

Creamed Onions

6 large onions, sliced

1 cup butter

2 teaspoons all-purpose flour

2 teaspoons salt

½ teaspoon white pepper

2 cups milk

In a large skillet or Dutch oven, sauté onions in butter until tender and golden brown, about 25 minutes. Remove with a slotted spoon. Add flour, salt and pepper to skillet; stir until smooth. Gradually stir in milk until blended. Bring to a boil; cook and stir for 2 minutes or until thickened. Reduce heat to medium. Return onions to the pan; heat through.

Mrs. Vicki's Onion-Roasted Potatoes

1 package onion soup mix

2 pounds potatoes, washed and peeled

⅓ cup oil

Preheat oven to 450°. Cut potatoes into cubes. In a large bowl, combine dry onion soup and oil. Add potatoes and coat evenly. Pour potatoes into a 9x13-inch dish. Bake 40 minutes, stirring occasionally, or until potatoes are tender.

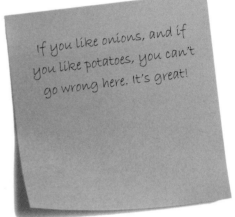

If you like onions, and if you like potatoes, you can't go wrong here. It's great!

Easy Au Gratin Potatoes

2 tablespoons butter

2 tablespoons flour

1 cup milk

⅛ teaspoon garlic powder

1 cup shredded cheese

2 cans new potatoes, drained and sliced

Melt butter in a saucepan. Blend in flour. Mix in milk and cook, stirring often, until thickened. Add garlic powder and ½ cup cheese. Mix potatoes and sauce in a 2-quart dish. Top with remaining cheese. Bake at 275° for 25 minutes or until brown.

Golden Potato Surprise

5 medium potatoes, peeled and diced

2 tablespoons butter

½ medium onion, chopped

2 tablespoons all-purpose flour

½ teaspoon thyme

½ teaspoon salt

½ teaspoon pepper

1 cup half and half

1 teaspoon Dijon mustard

½ cup mayonnaise

4 slices bacon, cooked and crumbled

Cook potatoes in boiling water until tender. Drain and set aside. Melt butter in a saucepan. Sauté onions until soft. Stir in flour, thyme, salt and pepper. Gradually add half and half, stirring often, until sauce thickens. Remove from heat; cool slightly. Add mustard and mayonnaise; stir well. Place potatoes in 1½-quart dish. Cover with sauce and bake at 350° for 30 minutes. Sprinkle with bacon just before serving.

istockphoto / Lauri Patterson

Cream Cheese Potatoes

2 pounds potatoes, peeled and cubed

1 (8-ounce) package cream cheese, cubed

2 tablespoons minced onion

¼ teaspoon garlic powder

1 teaspoon salt

¼ teaspoon black pepper

Boil Potatoes until tender. Drain and mash. Mix in cubed cream cheese, minced onion, garlic powder, salt and pepper. Stir well. Serve.

Twice Baked Potatoes

6 Russet potatoes, washed

1 (8-ounce) carton sour cream

3 green onions, chopped fine (optional)

½ package real bacon pieces

1 stick butter

1 cup shredded Cheddar cheese

Bake potatoes at 400° for 1 hour or until done; cool. Cut potatoes in half lengthwise and spoon inside of potato into a bowl (leave shell in tact). Add sour cream, onions, bacon and butter. Mix with an electric mixer until smooth. Fill potato skins with mixture and sprinkle with cheese. Bake at 400° another 20 minutes.

Meats & Main Dishes
**Beef • Pork
Chicken • Seafood**

Sloppy Joes

1 pound ground beef

½ cup chopped onion,

⅔ cup ketchup

1 tablespoon vinegar

1 tablespoon sugar

1 tablespoon mustard

1 tablespoon Worcestershire sauce

Salt and pepper to taste

Brown ground beef and onions. Drain. Stir in remaining ingredients. Simmer 20 minutes. Serve hot over your favorite bun.

istockphoto / Hannamariah

The Best Hamburgers

2 pounds ground beef

2 envelopes Lipton Onion Dry Soup Mix

Onion powder to taste

Garlic powder to taste

Lemon-pepper seasoning to taste

3 shakes soy sauce

1 cup dry Italian breadcrumbs

Mix all and shape into patties. Grill or fry about 5 to 8 minutes or until done. Top with Glazed Onions and Kumback Sauce.

Glazed Onions

2 tablespoons butter

1½ tablespoons sugar

1 pound onions, sliced

In a skillet, melt butter and stir in sugar. Add onions; cook, stirring frequently, until they start to brown. Drain on a paper towel.

Kumback Sauce

1 cup mayonnaise

⅓ cup ketchup

3 tablespoons yellow mustard

2 tablespoons spicy brown mustard

¼ cup Heinz 57 honey steak sauce

4 tablespoons lemon juice

3 teaspoons Worcestershire sauce

Salt and pepper to taste

Tony Chachere's seasoning to taste

Mix all together. Refrigerate 20 minutes before serving.

Texas Hash

3 large onions, sliced

1 large green bell pepper, minced

3 tablespoons oil

1 pound ground beef

1 cup uncooked rice

2 cups cooked tomatoes (or canned)

1 teaspoon chili powder

1 teaspoon salt

⅛ teaspoon black pepper

Sauté onions and peppers in oil until tender. Add ground beef and cook until brown; drain. Stir in remaining ingredients. Pour into greased 2-quart casserole dish. Cover and bake 1 hour at 350°. Remove cover for last 15 minutes of cook time.

Country-Style Meatloaf for Two

1 pound ground beef

1 egg, beaten

1 teaspoon sugar

Salt and pepper to taste

5 crackers, crumbled

½ onion, diced

1 small can tomato sauce

Ketchup

Mix all ingredients, except ketchup. Shape into a loaf and place in a loaf pan. Top with ketchup and bake at 350° for 1 hour.

Even though I have a family of four, this is one of my favorite recipes. I am the only one who likes meatloaf, so I take the left-over slice to work the next day.

Aunt Mary's Beefy Italian Mac &

1 pound ground beef

½ onion, chopped

Salt and pepper

2 (24-ounce) cans traditional spaghetti sauce

1 (15-ounce) can Italian-style diced tomatoes

1 pound elbow noodles

1 (1-pound) block Velveeta cheese, cubed

Brown hamburger meat with onion, salt and pepper; drain. Stir in spaghetti sauce and Italian style tomatoes. Boil elbow noodles as directed, drain. Stir noodles and cheese into meat mixture. Simmer until cheese has melted.

Traditional Tater Tot Casserole

1 pound ground beef

½ onion, chopped fine

Salt and pepper to taste

1 (32-ounce) bag tater tots

1 can cream of mushroom soup

1 can cream of chicken soup

4 ounces sour cream

½ cup milk

1 tablespoon butter, melted

2 cups shredded cheese

Brown meat with onions, salt and pepper; drain. Cover bottom of baking dish with meat, then layer with tater tots. In a separate bowl, mix both soups, milk, sour cream and butter; pour over tater tots. Top with cheese. Bake at 375° for 30 minutes.

Chili Pie

1 pound ground beef

1 (12-ounce) cans chili beans, drained

1 (15-ounce) can diced tomatoes

1 small onion, chopped fine

Salt and pepper to taste

1 tablespoon chili powder

Corn Chips

1½ cups shredded Cheddar cheese

Brown hamburger meat in a medium skillet; drain. Stir in beans, tomatoes, onions and seasonings. Cover and simmer 20 to 25 minutes. Serve over corn chips and topped with shredded cheese.

thinskstock / iStockphoto / Elena Rakhuba

Dinner in a Skillet

1 pound ground beef

Salt and pepper to taste

1 onion, chopped fine

1 medium bell pepper, diced

1 (10-ounce) can Ro-tel tomatoes

1 (15-ounce) can cream-style corn

1 (15-ounce) can whole-kernel corn

**1 package cornbread mix,
plus ingredients to prepare per directions**

Brown beef in a large, oven-safe skillet; drain. Season to taste with salt and pepper. Stir in onion, bell pepper, tomatoes, and corn. Bring to a boil then remove from heat. Mix cornbread according to package directions; spoon over beef mixture. DO NOT STIR. Bake at 350° until golden brown.

Beef

Pizza Casserole

1 pound ground beef

1 (15-ounce) can chunky Italian-style tomato sauce

1 (4-ounce) can sliced mushrooms, drained

1 (10-ounce) can refrigerated pizza dough

1 (8-ounce) package shredded mozzarella cheese, divided

Sliced Pepperoni to taste

In a 10-inch skillet, brown hamburger meat; drain. Add tomato sauce and mushrooms; stir. Press pizza crust into bottom and halfway up sides of a treated 9x13-inch baking dish. Sprinkle ½ mozzarella cheese crust. Top with meat mixture then a layer of pepperoni. Bake uncovered at 425° for 12 minutes. Top with remaining mozzarella cheese. Bake additional 5 minutes or until cheese is melted.

My kids, like most kids, love pizza. This is something a little different. They enjoy it, and the adults do too!

Stuffed Peppers

1½ pounds ground beef

3 tablespoons rice, uncooked

2 eggs, beaten

½ teaspoon salt

6 green bell peppers

1 (10¾-ounce) can condensed tomato soup

Combine meat, rice, eggs and salt; set aside. Cut tops off bell peppers and soak peppers in hot water about 2 minutes. Scoop out seeds and fill with meat mixture. Stand peppers in casserole dish. Pour tomato soup around peppers and bake at 300° for 1 hour.

If a bell pepper has three bumps on the bottom it is sweeter and better for eating raw. If it has four bumps on the bottom, it is likely firmer and better for cooking.

thinkstock / istockphoto / Ildiko Papp

Chimichangas

2 cups diced roast beef

1 small can green chiles

1 small onion, chopped

½ teaspoon cumin

Minced garlic to taste

1 beef bouillon cube

2 tablespoons cornstarch

1 package flour tortillas

Melted butter

Mozzarella cheese

Combine roast, chiles, onion, cumin, garlic, bouillon and cornstarch in a saucepan. Add water to barely cover and simmer until meat is fully cooked. Drain and wrap in flour tortillas. Place 1-inch apart on greased cookie sheet. Brush with melted butter. Bake at 350° until tortillas are brown. Top with cheese, and serve immediately.

Taco Pie

1 pound ground beef

1 package taco seasoning

1 cup thick and chunky picante sauce

1 egg, beaten

1 (9-inch) deep-dish pie crust

1½ cups shredded Monterey Jack cheese, divided

1 (4.5-ounce) can chopped green chiles

Brown meat; drain. Add taco seasoning and picante sauce. Simmer 5 to 8 minutes. Remove from heat and stir in egg. Sprinkle pie crust with ½ cup cheese and top with green chiles. Pour meat mixture over top and finish with remaining shredded cheese. Place pie pan on a baking sheet and bake at 350° for 20 to 25 minutes.

Tamale Pie

1 (15-ounce) can whole kernel corn, drained

1 (15-ounce) can tamales, chopped

1 (15-ounce) can chili without beans

2 cups shredded Cheddar cheese

Layer corn, tamales, chili and shredded cheese in a 2-quart casserole dish ending with a layer of cheese on top. Bake at 400° for 15 minutes. Serve hot.

Homemade Spanish Rice

½ pound ground beef

¼ cup chopped onion

1 tablespoon oil

¼ cup chopped green peppers

6 tablespoons long grain rice

1 teaspoon salt and pepper

1 (6-ounce) can tomato paste

2 cups hot water

Brown ground beef and onions in oil; drain. Return to skillet and add remaining ingredients. Cover and cook over low heat 20 minutes or until rice is tender. Stir occasionally.

On National Bosses Day, we had a surprise fiesta party for my boss, Sheila, because she loves Mexican Cuisine. I made this Homemade Spanish Rice, and everyone loved it. It's yummy topped with queso or on your tacos.

Enchilada Casserole

1 pound ground beef

1 medium onion, chopped

1 can cream of chicken soup

1 can cream of mushroom soup

1 can enchilada sauce

1 cup milk

1 can chopped green chile peppers

4 large flour tortillas

¼ pound Velveeta Shreds (pre-shredded Velveeta cheese)

Cook hamburger and onion; drain. Stir in both soups, enchilada sauce and milk; heat. Stir in green chiles. In a 9x13-inch greased casserole, layer ⅓ meat mixture, ½ cheese and 2 tortillas. Repeat layers then top with remaining meat mixture. Bake at 350° until bubbly, about 40 minutes.

istockphoto / James Pauls;

Mom's Roast Beef Dinner

1 (4-pound) beef chuck roast

4 Irish potatoes, peeled and chopped

1 bundle carrots, chopped

1 large onion, chopped

Salt and pepper to taste

1 (10½-ounce) can cream of mushroom soup

1 (10½-ounce) can cream of chicken soup

Place roast on heavy aluminum foil in a shallow pan. Layer potatoes, carrots and onions around roast; add salt and pepper. Top with soups. Wrap securely and bake at 450° for 15 minutes; then bake at 250° for 3½ hours.

Coca-Cola Brisket

1 envelope onion soup mix

1 (12-ounce) can regular Coca Cola

1 (10-ounce) bottle A-1 steak sauce

1 teaspoon black pepper

1 (6-pound) brisket, trimmed

Combine onion soup mix, Coca Cola, A-1 steak sauce and pepper; mix well. Place brisket fat side up in a large pan. Pour sauce over brisket and bake covered at 325° for 5 hours, or until brisket is tender.

Chicken Fried Steak

2 pounds boneless round steak

1 cup all-purpose flour

1 teaspoon season salt

1 teaspoon pepper

½ teaspoon garlic salt

2 eggs

¼ cup milk

Vegetable oil

Tenderize steak with a meat mallet. Cut into bite-sized pieces. Combine flour with seasonings. Combine eggs and milk; beat well. Heat 1 inch of oil in a skillet to 375°. While oil is heating, coat steak with flour, dip into egg mixture, and then coat flour mixture again. Fry steak in hot oil until browned, turning steak only once. Drain on paper towels. Reserve ¼ pan drippings for gravy.

Cream Gravy

¼ cup pan drippings

¼ cup flour

2 to 3 cups milk

½ teaspoon salt

¼ teaspoon pepper

Add flour to pan drippings; cook over medium heat until bubbly, stirring constantly. Add milk a little at a time; cook until thickened. Stir in salt and pepper. Serve Chicken Fried Steak topped with Cream Gravy.

Corned Beef Hash

1 onion, chopped

Oil

5 potatoes, peeled and cubed

1 can corned beef hash

Salt and pepper to taste

Garlic powder to taste

Sauté onions in small amount of oil; add potatoes. Cover and cook on low until potatoes are done. Add remaining ingredients; stir. Cover and cook an additional 5 minutes.

Corndogs

¼ cup cornmeal

¾ cup flour

1 tablespoon sugar

1 egg

½ cup milk

1 package hot dogs

Oil for frying

Popsicle sticks

In a bowl, mix cornmeal, flour and sugar. In a separate bowl, beat eggs and milk. Combine with flour mixture; mix well. Dip hot dogs in batter and coat well. Deep fry until golden brown; drain on a paper towel. Cool, then stick a Popsicle stick in one end of corndog.

These homemade corndogs are actually cheaper to make yourself than to buy. My kids love them.

Sour Cream & Onion Pork

4 boneless pork chops

Salt and pepper

2 tablespoons vegetable oil

2 medium sweet onions, separated into rings

1 cup beef stock

1 teaspoon yellow mustard

1 teaspoon paprika

1 (8-ounce) carton sour cream

4 to 6 cups cooked rice, optional

Season pork chops with salt and pepper to taste. In a large skillet, heat oil over medium-high heat. Add pork chops and cook until browned, 4 to 5 minutes per side. Cover pork chops with onion rings. In a small bowl, combine beef stock, mustard and paprika; season to taste with salt and pepper. Pour over pork chops. Bring mixture to a boil then reduce heat to medium and cook 30 minutes, stirring occasionally. Stir in sour cream until well-blended and cook just until heated through, about 5 minutes; do not boil. Serve over hot cooked rice if desired.

French Onion Chops

4 boneless pork chops

2 packages dry french onion soup mix

½ cup breadcrumbs

3 eggs

Preheat oven to 400°. In a shallow dish, combine soup mix and breadcrumbs. Beat eggs in a separate dish. Dip pork chops in egg then coat well with breadcrumb mixture. Place pork chops on a baking sheet and bake 10 minutes; flip and bake an additional 10 minutes.

Pork Chop Casserole

6 pork chops

1 stick butter

Salt and pepper

½ cup chopped onions

¼ cup chopped bell peppers

1 can cream of mushroom soup

1 cup rice

In a skillet, brown pork chops in butter. Remove from skillet, and season with salt and pepper. Add onion and bell pepper to skillet; sauté until soft but not brown. Blend cream of mushroom soup and 1 soup can of water in a blender. Pour into skillet. Add rice and simmer 1 minute. Pour into an oblong pan and place pork chops on top. Cover with foil. Bake in oven at 350° for 45 minutes.

Smothered Pork Chops

4 (1-inch-think) center-cut pork chops

Salt, pepper and cayenne pepper

2 tablespoons butter

¼ cup all-purpose flour

2 medium green bell peppers, sliced

2 medium onions, sliced

1 garlic clove, minced

2 cups chicken broth

2 to 3 dashes Worcestershire sauce

Trim fat from chops and season to taste with salt, pepper, and cayenne. Melt butter in a skillet over medium heat. Place flour in a plate and roll chops in flour. Shake to remove excess flour then place in skillet. Brown well, about 3 minutes per side; remove to a plate and set aside. Add bell peppers and onions to skillet, and saute until softened, about 3 minutes. Stir in garlic and cook slightly, about a minute. Push vegetables to side of skillet. Return pork chops to pan and cover with vegetables. Pour broth over top and sprinkle with Worcestershire sauce. Cover pan and simmer 45 minutes or until chops are tender.

Creamy Potato Pork Chops

8 medium potatoes, peeled and sliced

½ medium onion, minced

Salt and pepper to taste

White Sauce

1 cup all-purpose flour

2 tablespoons seasoned salt

⅓ cup vegetable oil

8 boneless pork chops

Preheat oven to 350°. Spread ½ potatoes in a well-greased large (10x15-inch) casserole dish. Layer with ½ onions. Season with salt and pepper. Repeat layers. Top with white sauce. Heat oil to sizzling over medium-high heat. Season pork chops with seasoned salt and coat with flour. Lightly brown chops in vegetable oil. (Don't worry about getting them done; they will finish cooking in the oven.) Lay pork chops over potatoes. Cover with aluminum foil and bake 30 minutes. Uncover and bake another 30 minutes or until potatoes are tender.

White Sauce

1 stick butter

½ cup all-purpose flour

4 cups milk

2 teaspoons salt

¾ teaspoon pepper

Melt butter over medium heat; quickly stir in flour, salt and pepper. Cook, stirring constantly, until hot. Add milk slowly, 1 cup at a time, whisking continuously. Bring to a boil, stirring frequently. Reduce heat and simmer 2 minutes. Remove from heat and immediately pour over potatoes.

BBQ Pork Ribs

2 pounds pork ribs

1 cup orange juice

1 (12-ounce) bottle barbecue sauce

Preheat oven to 300°. Place ribs in a 9x13-inch baking dish. Whisk together orange juice (fresh is best) and barbecue sauce. Pour sauce over ribs; coating entirely. Cover tightly with foil. Bake three hours (NO PEEKING). Remove foil and increase temperature to 350°. Bake 1 additional hour, turning after 30 minutes.

Golden Fried Pork Chops

4 to 6 thin pork chops

1 to 2 teaspoons seasoned salt

1 egg

2 tablespoons milk

½ cup flour

1 to 2 tablespoons vegetable oil

Sprinkle pork chops with seasoned salt; rub seasoning into meat. Beat egg and milk. Dip each pork chop into flour, then into egg mixture and back into flour. Place in skillet of hot oil and cook on medium-high 5 minutes per side until golden brown.

Do a lot of frying but hate the spattering grease? Use your sifter to sift a little flour over the hot fat and the spattering will disappear! Just a little flour else you will have a sloppy mess. Or, turn a metal colander or strainer upside down over the skillet. This allows the steam to escape and keeps fat from spattering.

Maw-Maw Lisa's Pork Loin

1 small to medium pork loin

Butter, softened

1 package onion soup mix

Black pepper to taste

¼ cup water

Rub butter over pork loin until completely covered. Roll into dry onion soup mix and sprinkle lightly with pepper over full surface of pork loin. Pour water in bottom of casserole dish. Place pork loin fat-side-up in casserole dish. Bake at 350° for 20 minutes per pound.

Every Thanksgiving and every Christmas, Maw-Maw Lisa makes her pork loin. If she doesn't, the entire family usually gets upset. It's the best and always so juicy.

Kathy's Pulled Pork

1 Boston butt pork roast

Salt and pepper to taste

Crushed red pepper to taste

1 (16-ounce) bottle barbecue sauce

Wash roast. While roast is still damp season with salt, pepper and crushed red peppers. In a crockpot, cook on high 8 hours. Remove excess fat from roast; shred meat. Mix in barbecue sauce.

Tory's Spaghetti Carbonara

1 (16-ounce) package spaghetti noodles

3 teaspoons olive oil, divided

1 pound bacon, diced

1 cup diced ham or prosciutto

1 bunch green onions, chopped

1 large ripe tomato, diced

1 bunch fresh parsley, chopped

1 cup frozen green peas

1 cup heavy cream

1 cup freshly grated Parmesan

2 egg yolks

Boil spaghetti noodles in water with 1 teaspoon olive oil until al dente; drain and reserve to a large serving bowl. Add remaining to 2 teaspoons olive oil to a large skillet. Fry bacon until crispy; do not drain grease. Add ham, green onions, tomato, parsley and green peas. Stir well. In a separate bowl, mix together cream, Parmesan cheese and egg yolks. When bacon mixture is really hot, pour it over pasta. Toss until pasta is covered. Add cream mixture. Stir well.

thinkstock / istockphoto

Potato and Sausage Casserole

1 (1-pound) package smoked sausage, thinly sliced

1 small onion, chopped fine

4 medium potatoes, peeled and cubed

Salt and pepper

In a large skillet, brown sausage with onions; add potatoes. Cover and cook over medium-low heat until potatoes are tender. Season to taste with salt and pepper; serve.

Mama's Red Beans & Rice

5 cups water

1 (16-ounce) bag long grain white rice

¼ cup frozen chopped onions

1 (15-ounce) can chili beans

1 (15-ounce) can red kidney beans

1 (8-ounce) can tomato sauce

1 pound chopped sausage

5 bouillon beef cubes

Dash garlic salt

Dash onion salt

Dash Tony Chachere's Cajun Seasoning

Salt and pepper to taste

In a large boiler, combine all ingredients. Bring to a rolling boil. Reduce heat; cover. Simmer 20 minutes or until rice is tender.

This is the first recipe Mama and I made together. That's a very special moment in my life—cooking alongside my mother.

Key West Chicken

¼ pound (1 stick) butter

1 whole chicken, skinned and chopped

1 teaspoon salt

1 teaspoon freshly ground pepper

¼ teaspoon paprika

1 large onion, thinly sliced

3 to 4 cloves garlic, crushed

¼ cup Key lime juice

Melt butter over medium heat in large frying pan with cover. Add chicken and cook until light brown on all sides. Sprinkle with salt, pepper and paprika. Add onion and garlic. Cook 5 minutes, stirring occasionally. Pour lime juice over chicken. Cover and simmer 25 minutes or until fork can be inserted with ease. Remove cover, and cook a few minutes until chicken is a golden color.

Chicken

Oven Fried Chicken

2 pounds cut-up chicken

5 tablespoons butter, melted

¼ cup flour

2 teaspoons dry mustard

1 teaspoon paprika

Salt and pepper

Pour melted butter in a large baking dish. In a large zip-lock bag combine flour, mustard, paprika, salt and pepper. Place chicken in bad, one at time, and shake. Lay chicken in buttered baking dish, flipping once to roll in butter. Bake at 350° for 35 minutes. Turn once. Increase oven temperature to 450° and bake additional 10 to 15 minutes.

Southern Fried Chicken

1 chicken fryer, cut up

2 cups buttermilk

2 eggs, beaten

1½ cups flour

Salt and pepper to taste

Onion powder to taste

Garlic powder to taste

Season salt to taste

2 cups Crisco shortening

Wash chicken and pat dry. Place in a large bowl of buttermilk and egg. Refrigerate at least 6 hours. Drain chicken. Season flour with salt, pepper, onion powder, garlic powder and season salt. Flour chicken 1 piece at a time. In a Dutch oven, heat shortening on medium-high. Place chicken in hot shortening and fry uncovered about 15 minutes. Flip chicken and cover with lid, venting just enough for steam to escape. Fry additional 15 minutes; drain on paper towels.

Breading on the chicken stays on the chicken. Well, it will if you follow this easy tip. Transfer your breaded chicken pieces to a baking rack set over a baking sheet, and allow them to dry about 5 minutes. This brief drying time stabilizes the coating so that it won't stick to the pan or fall off.

Krystal's Crunchy Chicken Casserole

1 chicken, boiled and deboned

1 can cream of mushroom soup

1 can cream of celery soup

1 (16-ounce) can Ro-Tel tomatoes, well drained (optional)

1 (8-ounce) carton sour cream

1 can water chestnuts

2 cups shredded Cheddar cheese

1 sleeve Ritz crackers, crushed

1 stick margarine, melted

Chop boiled chicken and layer in a greased baking dish. Combine soups, tomatoes, sour cream and water chestnuts; pour over chicken. Top with shredded cheese. Pour crushed crackers on top. Drizzle melted butter over crackers. Bake at 350° for 35 minutes.

Chicken

Krystal Babb said she serves this dish when company's coming. I say cook it anytime. It's great and everyone loves it.

Chicken & Rice Casserole

1 whole chicken fryer

2 cups rice

1 can cream of mushroom soup

1 can cream of chicken soup

1 large onion, sliced

1 can mushrooms

1 tablespoon salt

1 teaspoon pepper

Wash chicken well, cut into pieces, and set aside. Mix uncooked rice with soups. Pour in baking dish and layer onions and mushrooms over the top. Lay chicken on top and season to taste with salt and pepper. Cover with aluminum foil and bake at 350° for 45 minutes to 1 hour until chicken is done.

French Dressing Baked Chicken

1 whole chicken, cut up

1 (8-ounce) bottle French salad dressing

1 package dry onion soup mix

Place chicken in 9x13-inch baking dish. Mix together dressing and dry soup mix; pour over chicken. Bake uncovered at 350° for 1 hour and 20 minutes.

Easy Six-Can Casserole

2 (9- to 12-ounce) cans canned chicken breast

1 (10½-ounce) can cream of celery soup

1 (10½-ounce) can cream of mushroom soup

1 (4-ounce) can mushrooms, drained

1 cup diced celery

1 can chow mein noodles

Combine all ingredients except noodles. Pour into a buttered casserole dish. Top with noodles. Bake at 325° for 1 hour.

Easy Chicken Noodle Dish

2 chicken breasts, cubed

3 cups wide egg noodles

1 (10½-ounce) can cream of chicken soup

⅛ teaspoon pepper

½ cup milk

2 hard-boiled eggs, chopped

⅓ cup shredded cheese (optional)

Boil chicken in 6 cups water. Remove chicken and set aside; reserve broth. Boil noodles in reserved chicken broth until tender; drain. In a separate bowl, mix together cream of chicken soup, pepper, milk, chicken and noodles. Pour into a 9x13-inch baking dish. Bake at 350° for 30 minutes; stir after about 15 minutes. When done stir in eggs and top with cheese.

Easy Chicken Alfredo

2 boneless skinless chicken breasts, boiled

1 (12-ounce) package egg noodles

1 jar alfredo sauce

1 can cream of chicken soup

Boil chicken in 5 cups water. Remove chicken and set aside. Boil egg noodles until the water boils down low. Add cream of chicken soup and Alfredo sauce; mix well. Add the noodles to the chicken and pour into a casserole dish. Top with sauce. Bake at 350° until sauce is bubbly.

thinkstock / istockphoto / Charles Brutlag

Chicken Roll-Ups

8 boneless skinless chicken breast halves

2 tablespoons butter

Salt and pepper

Garlic powder

Onion powder

2 packages cream cheese, softened

1 package dry Italian seasoning mix

2 (8-ounce) cans crescent rolls (keep refrigerated until ready to use)

Sauté chicken in butter until meat turns white, and then season to taste. Preheat oven at 350°. Mix cream cheese with dry Italian seasoning. Shred chicken and mix with cream cheese mixture. Unroll crescent rolls and spread 2 tablespoons chicken mixture on each crescent roll. Roll up starting with long end first. Bake on a treated 9x13-inch casserole pan for 10 to 15 minutes, or until tops of crescent rolls are browned.

Easy Chicken Pot Pie

1 whole chicken

2 pie crusts

1 large can Veg-All, drained

1 stick butter

Flour

Boil and debone chicken reserving broth. Place 1 pie crust in a 9x13-inch baking dish. Layer chicken then Veg-All on top of crust. Melt butter in a medium heavy pot. Add enough flour to make a paste. With a whisk slowly add 3 cups chicken broth until blended well. Cook over medium-low heat until thickens. Pour over Veg-All. Place remaining pie crust over top. Poke holes with fork in pie crust. Bake at 350° until crust is browned and bubbly.

Chicken Crescents

4 cups cooked chopped chicken

½ small onion, finely chopped

½ cup finely chopped celery

2 tablespoons butter, melted

6 ounces cream cheese

2 cans crescent rolls

Salt and pepper to taste

Cook celery and onions in butter until soft but not brown. Add cream cheese and chicken and cook just until cheese is melted and chicken is hot. Separate crescents rolls, keeping two together so you have squares. Top each square with even amounts chicken filling. Bring the four corners of the filled roll together to make a bundle. Bake on a treated cookie sheet at 350° about 20 minutes or until brown.

Gravy

¼ cup milk

2 cups cream of chicken soup

Cook slowly for 6 minutes stirring to mix well. Pour gravy over each bundle when serving.

Easy Chicken Pie

1 whole chicken

1 stick butter

1 can cream of mushroom soup

Salt and pepper to taste

1 (10-count) can biscuits

Boil chicken until tender; remove from bone and layer in square dish. Cut 1 stick of butter over chicken. Mix soup with a 3 tablespoons water; add salt and pepper to taste and pour over chicken. Pull each biscuit in half and layer over soup mixture. Bake at 350° for 25 minutes or until biscuits are done.

Laura's Chicken Enchiladas

5 to 6 chicken breasts, boiled and deboned

1 medium jar mild Pace picante sauce

Salt and pepper to taste

Onion powder to taste, optional

2 (10½-ounce) cans cream of chicken soup

1 (14- to 16-ounce) can chicken broth

1 (8-ounce) carton sour cream

¼ stick margarine

1 (10-count) package big flour tortillas

2 cups shredded mild Cheddar and mozzarella cheese mix

Shred boiled chicken and mix with picante sauce; add salt, pepper and onion powder to taste. In a medium saucepan, blend soup, broth, sour cream and margarine; heat. Pour enough in bottom of casserole disk just to cover bottom. Warm tortillas in microwave (makes them easier to roll). Fill tortillas with chicken and put some cheese on top. Put enchiladas in pan and pour remaining sauce on top, top with remaining cheese. Bake at 400° for about 20 minutes.

thinkstock / istockphoto / Olga Nayashkova

Corn Tortilla Chicken Lasagna

36 (6-inch) corn tortillas

6 cups shredded or cubed cooked chicken breast

1 (28-ounce) can kidney beans, rinsed and drained

1 (16-ounce) can kidney beans, rinsed and drained

3 (16-ounce) jars salsa

3 cups (24 ounces) sour cream

3 large green bell peppers, chopped

3 (3.8-ounce) cans sliced ripe olives, drained

3 cups (12 ounces) shredded Monterey Jack cheese

3 cups (12 ounces) shredded Cheddar cheese

In each of 2 greased 9x13-inch dishes, arrange 6 tortillas. Layer each with 1 cup chicken, ⅔ cup kidney beans, 1 cup salsa, ½ cup sour cream, ½ cup bell pepper, about ⅓ cup olives, ½ cup Monterey Jack cheese and ½ cup Cheddar cheese. Repeat layers twice. Cover and bake at 350° for 25 minutes. Uncover; bake 10 to 15 minutes longer or until cheese is melted. Let stand 10 minutes before serving.

Doritos Chicken Casserole

4 boneless, skinless chicken breasts

1 can cream of celery soup

1 can cream of chicken soup

1 can cream of mushroom soup

1 can cream of onion soup

1 can Ro-Tel tomatoes

1 bag Doritos (nacho cheese flavored)

2 cups shredded Cheddar cheese

Boil chicken until done. In a separate boiler, boil all soups and Ro-Tel (juice included). Remove from heat. Cut chicken into small squares. Stir into soup mixture. In a greased casserole dish crush Doritos and layer in bottom of dish. Pour chicken and soup mixture over Doritos and top with cheese. Bake at 400° about 20 minutes or until cheese is melted and bubbly all over.

Las Vegas Chicken

6 slices Canadian bacon

6 chicken breasts

6 strips bacon

Salt and pepper

1 can cream of mushroom soup

1 (8-ounce) carton sour cream

Lay Canadian bacon in bottom of a treated casserole dish. Salt and pepper chicken and wrap each with a slice of bacon. Lay over Canadian bacon. Mix together soup and sour cream and pour over chicken. Bake uncovered at 275° for 3½ hours.

Quick & Easy Chicken

2 boneless skinless chicken breasts, boiled

1 can cream of chicken soup

½ cup milk

¼ cup mayonnaise

1 can chow mein noodles

Chop boiled chicken and set aside. Mix soup, milk and mayonnaise until smooth. Carefully stir in chow mein noodles and chicken. Bake at 350° for 25 minutes or until bubbly.

Poppy Seed Chicken

6 boneless, skinless chicken breasts

1 can cream of chicken soup

1 can cream of mushroom soup

1 (8-ounce) carton sour cream

2 tablespoons poppy seeds

1 cup shredded cheese

1 sleeve Ritz crackers, crushed

½ stick butter, melted

Boil chicken until meat turns white; cube into small pieces. Mix chicken, soups, sour cream, poppy seeds and cheese. Stir well, and pour into a baking dish. Mix together crushed crackers and melted butter. Pour over chicken mixture. Bake at 350° for 45 minutes or until hot and bubbly.

In the South, everyone loves Poppy Seed Chicken. This recipe is really good and really simple. It's one of my son Christian's favorite dinners.

thinkstock / istockphoto / massimiliano gallo

Sesame Chicken Breasts

10 boneless skinless chicken breasts

1 cup sour cream

2 tablespoons lemon juice

2 teaspoons Worcestershire sauce

2 teaspoons celery salt

1 teaspoon paprika

½ teaspoon black pepper

1 teaspoon seasoned salt

½ teaspoon lemon pepper

Dash Tabasco sauce

2 sticks margarine, divided

2 tablespoons sesame seeds

2 cups Italian-flavored breadcrumbs

Rinse chicken breasts and set aside. Mix sour cream, lemon juice, Worcestershire sauce, celery salt, paprika, black pepper, seasoned salt, lemon pepper and dash of Tabasco. Place chicken in mixture beings sure each is covered completely. Refrigerate overnight. The next day remove chicken breast from mixture. In a separate bowl, melt 1 stick margarine and mix with sesame seeds and bread crumbs. Roll each chicken breast in breadcrumbs mixture. Place on a lightly greased pan. Melt remaining stick margarine and spoon ½ over chicken. Bake at 350°, uncovered, for 45 minutes. Spoon remaining margarine over chicken. Bake 20 to 25 minutes longer. Enjoy.

Better than Dumplings

2 to 3 chicken breasts

1 can cream of mushroom

½ cup melted butter

Salt and pepper

½ cup flour

½ cup milk

Boil chicken until done. Drain, reserving 1 cup chicken broth. Allow chicken to cool; shred chicken. Mix 1 cup reserved chicken broth with soup. Pour butter in a casserole dish. Spread shredded chicken over butter; season to taste. Spread soup mixture over chicken. Mix flour and milk together and pour over top of mixture. Bake at 375° until golden brown, about 30 to 35 minutes.

Chicken & Dumplings

4 chicken breasts, boiled

1 (10½-ounce) can cream of chicken soup

1 can biscuits

3 tablespoons butter

Salt and pepper to taste

½ cup milk

Boil chicken in 4 cups water. Reserving broth, remove chicken and shred fine. In a medium saucepan, stir soup and chicken into reserved broth; bring to a rolling boil. Separate biscuits and cut in half. Roll into balls. Drop into boiling broth. Add butter, salt and pepper; stir. Reduce heat and cover. Cook 10 to 15 minutes. Stir in milk just before serving.

Krista's Easy Chicken Quesadillas

1 pound chicken strips

¼ cup chopped onions

1 can hot or mild Ro-Tel tomatoes

1 package flour tortillas

2 cups shredded Cheddar cheese

1 (8-ounce) container sour cream

Cajun seasoning, optional

In a greased non-stick skillet, cook chicken until done. Add onions and Ro-Tel tomatoes; simmer 10 minutes. Heat tortillas one at a time in a non-stick skillet. Sprinkle each tortilla with cheese. Top with chicken mixture. Garnish with sour cream (mixed with Cajun seasoning, if desired). Fold tortilla to serve. Also good made with black beans.

I made these Chicken Quesadillas one evening when my husband and my father-in-law were headed back from deer camp. I needed something quick, and these were delicious, too. The men ate every bite.

istockphoto / Joe Gough

Chicken Spaghetti with a Kick

4 to 6 boneless, skinless chicken breasts

Salt and pepper

1 (24-ounce) package spaghetti noodles

2 pounds Velveeta cheese, cubed

1 large onion, chopped

1 large bell pepper, chopped

1 stick margarine or butter

2 cans medium or hot Ro-Tel tomatoes

1 can English peas, drained well

Salt and pepper to taste

Boil chicken until meat turns white; reserve broth. Boil noodles in broth; drain. Add Velveeta to spaghetti and stir until melted and creamy. Sauté onion and pepper in margarine. Add to spaghetti along with chicken, Ro-Tel tomatoes, peas, salt and pepper. Bake at 350° for 30 minutes.

C.B.R. Spaghetti

1 (8-ounce) package angel hair spaghetti noodles

1 (10½-ounce) can cream of mushroom soup

1 boneless skinless chicken breast, cooked and chopped

½ cup real bacon pieces

½ cup buttermilk ranch dressing

Boil noodles as directed; drain. Stir in cream of mushroom soup, chopped chicken breast, bacon pieces and ranch. Stir well. Heat on low heat for 10 minutes or until heated thoroughly.

Dusty's Favorite Chicken Spaghetti

3 boneless, skinless chicken breasts

1 (32-ounce) block Velveeta cheese, cubed

1 (10-ounce) can mild or medium Ro-Tel tomatoes

1 (10.5-ounce) can cream of chicken soup

2 (10.5-ounce) cans cream of mushroom soup

1 (16-ounce) package angel hair noodles

1 tablespoon butter

3 tablespoons milk

Salt and pepper

Boil chicken breast in 5 cups water. Remove chicken when done and cube and set aside in a separate bowl. Cook noodles in chicken broth for 3 minutes; drain. In a large boiler, combine all ingredients. Heat on low until cheese has thoroughly melted and becomes hot and bubbly.

My husband, Dusty, loves chicken spaghetti. I love making this just to see him smile. He says he can eat a pound of this in one sitting. Even though he usually doesn't, he does finish it up for breakfast. If Dusty had his way, I would make this every day.

Pulled Barbecue Chicken

6 to 8 boneless skinless chicken breasts

1 cup ketchup

⅓ cup Worcestershire

½ cup brown sugar

½ teaspoon garlic powder

Salt and pepper to taste

½ teaspoon onion powder

1 tablespoon butter

½ cup water

1 small onion, chopped (optional)

Place chicken in a crockpot. In a large bowl, whisk together all remaining ingredients. Pour over chicken. Cover and cook on low 6 to 8 hours, stirring about every 3 hours. Shred chicken with a fork.

Creamy Chicken Breasts

8 boneless skinless chicken breasts

Lemon pepper to taste

1 (10¾-ounce) can cream of chicken soup

1 (3-ounce) package cream cheese, softened

1 (8-ounce) carton sour cream

Cooked rice

Place 4 chicken breasts in the bottom of a crockpot. Sprinkle with lemon pepper. In a separate bowl mix chicken soup, sour cream and cream cheese in a bowl. Stir well. Pour half of the sauce over the 4 chicken breasts. Place remaining chicken breast over that. Top with other ½ of the sauce mixture. Cover and cook on high 4 hours. Serve over rice.

Simple & Delicious Chicken Breasts

4 boneless skinless chicken breasts

1 (10¾-ounce) can golden mushroom soup

1 envelope dry onion soup mix

Rinse chicken and put in the bottom of a crockpot. Pour golden mushroom soup over chicken. Sprinkle dry onion mix over the top. Cook on low 4 to 6 hours.

State Fair Chicken on a Stick

4 boneless skinless chicken breasts

1 onion

1 bell pepper

1 (16-ounce) bottle Italian dressing

Flour

Salt and pepper

Hamburger dill pickles

Kabob sticks

Cut chicken into squares. Cut onion and bell peppers into large pieces. Marinate chicken, onion and bell pepper in Italian dressing 1 to 2 hours. Pour some flour in a large zip-lock bag; season with salt and pepper. Drain chicken, onion, and bell peppers. Working in batches, place chicken, bell peppers, onion and pickles in bag with flour and shake to coat well. Layer, in that order, on kabob sticks repeating until stick is almost full. Deep fry until golden brown.

The Mississippi State Fair is October's biggest event in the state. Chicken on a Stick is one of the most sought after foods at the fair. This is about as close as you can get to having the real thing.

Louisiana Buffalo Wings

2½ pounds chicken wings, tips removed

1 stick margarine

⅓ cup Louisiana hot sauce

2 packages dry Italian salad dressing mix

½ teaspoon dry basil

Wash and dry chicken wings. Fry in hot oil until brown, using no flour. Melt margarine and mix with remaining ingredients. Dip browned wings in mixture and bake in a 9x13-inch baking pan at 350° for 10 to 20 minutes.

Chicken

istockphoto / Jack Puccio

Mushroom Chicken

6 skinless chicken legs

Salt and pepper

½ cup chicken broth

1 (10¾-ounce) can cream of mushroom

1 (4-ounce) can sliced mushrooms, drained

Wash chicken and pat dry. Salt and pepper chicken. Place in a greased 9x13-inch baking dish about ½ an inch apart. In a small bowl, mix broth with mushroom soup and stir well. Pour over chicken legs. Top with sliced mushrooms. Bake at 350° for 1 hour or until chicken is all white in the middle.

Tony's Grilled Mesquite Chicken

½ cup soy sauce

½ cup canola oil

¼ cup light brown sugar

¼ cup lemon juice

Dash pepper

4 chicken breasts

Combine all ingredients except chicken in a blender. Mix well. Place chicken in a Tupperware bowl with lid. Cover with marinade. Refrigerate 4 to 6 hours. When ready to cook, remove chicken from marinade. Discard marinade. Grill chicken until done.

Get your grill piping hot and take an onion half and stick it in the prongs of a long handled fork scrub the grates of your grill and it will become clean.

Tracy's Shrimp Gravy

1 (16-ounce) bottle Italian dressing

1 tablespoon Worcestershire sauce

1 large bag pre-cooked shrimp, thawed

1 tablespoon minced garlic

1 can sliced mushrooms

Juice of 6 lemons

2 sticks butter

Black pepper to taste

Preheat oven to 350°. In a 9x13-inch baking dish, combine all ingredients. Bake 20 minutes. Serve over Texas toast or rice.

Shrimp & Grits

3 cups yellow grits

2 cups heavy cream

1 stick butter

Garlic powder to taste

1 pound sharp Cheddar cheese, shredded

3 pounds raw shrimp, peeled and deveined

Preheat oven to 350°. Cook grits according to package directions using cream for the liquid. Stir in remaining ingredients. Pour into a greased 9x13-inch baking dish; cover and bake 20 minutes.

Shrimp Scampi

½ cup butter

5 cloves garlic, minced

2 tablespoons lemon juice

2 tablespoons chopped fresh parsley

1 pound medium shrimp, peeled

Cajun seasoning to taste

Place butter, garlic, lemon juice, and parsley in medium skillet. Cook, uncovered, over medium- high heat, about 4 minutes or until butter has melted. Add shrimp; stir well. Sprinkle with Cajun seasoning. Cook until shrimp are pink. Remove from heat to rest 5 minutes before serving.

thinkstock / istockphoto

Shrimp Fried Rice

1 cup chopped green pepper

1 cup chopped celery

¾ cup chopped onion

1 small garlic clove, chopped

5 tablespoons margarine

1 small can mushrooms, drained

1 pound cooked shrimp

4 cups cold cooked minute rice

4 tablespoons soy sauce

2 tablespoons chopped pimentos, optional

Sauté green pepper, celery, onion and garlic in margarine 5 minutes; add remaining ingredients and heat thoroughly.

Golden Fried Shrimp

4 pounds large peeled shrimp

1½ teaspoons Cajun seasoning

1 teaspoon black pepper

8 eggs, beaten

1½ cups flour

Season shrimp with Cajun seasoning and pepper in a large bowl; stir to coat. In a medium bowl, blend eggs with flour. Coat shrimp with egg batter; deep fry until golden brown.

Cocktail Sauce

1 cup ketchup

1 tablespoon lemon juice

4 tablespoons horseradish

1 teaspoon Worcestershire

¼ teaspoon onion powder

Dash Tabasco sauce or to taste

Mix all ingredients well. Store in air-tight container in refrigerator until ready to use.

Butter Sauce

½ cup butter

6 tablespoons lemon juice

Salt and pepper

1 teaspoon Worcestershire sauce

Melt butter in a small saucepan. Stir in remaining ingredients; heat well. Serve with shrimp or vegetables.

Summer-Time Boiled Shrimp

1 pound Cajun-style linked sausage

1 (6-ounce) package dry crab boil

6 cups water

6 ears fresh corn

1 package sliced portabella mushrooms

3 pounds shrimp

Salt and pepper

Slice sausage into ½-inch pieces. Place sausage and crab boil in water and boil about 30 minutes. Add corn and boil 6 minutes. Stir in mushrooms. Add more water if needed to keep ingredients completely covered. Bring back to a boil. Add shrimp; season with salt and pepper. Boil 3 minutes, stirring occasionally. Drain. For a larger crowd, double ingredients. Serve with cocktail sauce or butter sauce.

Seafood

thinkstock / istockphoto / Danny Hooks

Seafood Casserole

White Sauce

4 tablespoons butter

4 tablespoons flour

2 cups milk

1 teaspoon salt

Pepper to taste

In a medium saucepan, melt butter over low heat and stir in flour. Gradually add in milk; mix well. Add salt and pepper to taste. Stir constantly until sauce has thickened.

Casserole

3 hard-boiled eggs, sliced

1 cup tuna fish

⅔ cup precooked salad shrimp

1 cup cooked crabmeat

1 cup canned sliced mushrooms, drained

1 cup shredded American cheese

Salt to taste

White Sauce

1 cup dry breadcrumbs

¼ cup melted butter

Arrange eggs in bottom of treated casserole dish. Cover with tuna, shrimp and crabmeat. Add mushrooms, cheese, and salt to taste. Pour White Sauce over top. Mix breadcrumbs and butter and sprinkle over top. Bake at 350° for 35 minutes.

Crawfish Casserole

1 pound crawfish tails

½ pound crabmeat

1 can cream of mushroom soup

1 can cream of celery soup

4 tablespoons melted butter

1½ cups chicken broth

½ cup chopped bell pepper

Garlic salt to taste

Mix all ingredients; pour into a 9x13-inch casserole pan and bake covered for 1 hour at 350°. Serve over pasta or rice.

Tuna Dinner

1 (14-ounce) box Deluxe Macaroni and Cheese Dinner

½ cup milk

1 (10¾-ounce) can cream of mushroom soup

1 (6-ounce) can tuna in oil, drained

1 (13¼-ounce) can sweet peas, drained

Prepare Deluxe Macaroni and Cheese Dinner as directed on package mixing while still in saucepan. Stir in milk and soup; mix well. Gently stir in tuna and peas. Continue to heat an additional 10 minutes or until heated through.

Crab Cakes

1 pound crabmeat

1 medium onion, finely chopped

3 green onions, chopped

1 tablespoon chopped pimentos

12 saltine crackers, crushed

1 egg, beaten

½ cup mayonnaise

1 tablespoon Worcestershire

Salt and pepper to taste

Tabasco to taste

Combine all ingredients in a bowl, gently mix and form into 2-inch patties. Bake at 350° for 20 to 25 minutes.

Mock Lobster Roll

4 hot dog buns or long rolls, split

1 pound imitation crabmeat, chopped into bite-size chunks

3 green onions, sliced (use both green and white portions)

Juice 1 lemon

2 tablespoons ranch dressing

5 to 7 dashes hot sauce

2 teaspoons black pepper

1 teaspoon Old Bay Seasoning

Salt, to taste

Parsley, to garnish

Lightly butter the rolls and gently toast in a toaster oven or in the oven. Meanwhile, carefully combine imitation crab, green onions, lemon juice, ranch dressing, hot sauce, black pepper, Old Bay and salt in a mixing bowl, as to not break up the meat. Heap spoonfuls of the crab mixture into the rolls and top with a sprinkle of parsley.

Salmon Patties

1 (16-ounce) can pink salmon

1 egg

⅓ cup minced onions

½ cup flour

1½ teaspoons baking powder

1½ cups shortening

Drain salmon, saving 2 tablespoons juice. Mix salmon, egg and onions until sticky. Stir in flour. Add baking powder to salmon juice and stir. Mix into salmon mixture. Form into small patties and fry in hot melted shortening until golden brown.

thinkstock / istockphoto / Elzbieta Sekowska

Beer-Battered Catfish

Tartar Sauce

2 cups mayonnaise

3 tablespoons sweet pickle relish

2 tablespoons hot sauce

1 teaspoon lemon juice

1 teaspoon paprika

Stir together all ingredients. Refrigerate until ready to use.

Fish

1 pound catfish fillets

1½ cups self-rising flour

⅓ cup fresh lemon juice

⅔ cup beer

¾ cup oil

Wash fish and pat dry. Coat with flour; set aside. Combine remaining flour with lemon juice and beer. Stir until smooth. Heat oil in a large skillet over medium-high heat until hot but not smoking. Meanwhile, dip fish in batter. Fry fish until golden brown. Drain on a paper towel. Serve with Tartar Sauce.

thinkstock / istockphoto / Charlotte Allen

Cheesy Catfish

½ to 1 cup Parmesan cheese

¼ cup flour

1 teaspoon paprika

½ teaspoon salt

½ teaspoon pepper

2 pounds catfish fillets

1 egg, slightly beaten

1 tablespoon milk

¼ cup margarine, melted

Preheat oven to 350°. Combine cheese, flour and seasonings. In a separate bowl, combine egg and milk. Dip catfish into egg mixture then dredge in cheese mixture. Place into baking dish. Pour margarine over top. Bake at 350° until golden brown.

Onion Baked Catfish

6 catfish fillets

½ teaspoon Creole seasoning

1 cup sour cream

1 cup mayonnaise

1 package ranch-style dry salad dressing mix

1 (6-ounce) can French fried onion rings

Preheat oven to 350°. Put fillets in a shallow bowl, and sprinkle them evenly with Creole seasoning. Set aside. In a small bowl, combine sour cream, mayonnaise, and salad dressing mix. Blend well. Process onion rings in a blender until finely crushed. Put these in another shallow bowl. Dip fillets first in sour cream mixture, then in crushed onion rings, coating evenly. Put fish in an ungreased shallow baking pan. Bake uncovered until fish flakes easily when tested with a fork, about 20 minutes.

Baked Catfish

¼ cup yellow cornmeal

¼ cup plain flour

¼ cup grated Parmesan cheese

1 teaspoon paprika

½ teaspoon salt

½ teaspoon pepper

1 egg white

2 tablespoons milk

4 catfish fillets

½ teaspoon sesame seeds

Butter-flavored cooking spray

Combine first 6 ingredients. Whisk egg and milk together. Dip fish in egg mixture then in cornmeal mixture. Place on foil-lined sheet treated with nonstick spray. Sprinkle with sesame seeds and coat with cooking spray; bake at 350° for 30 minutes or until flaky.

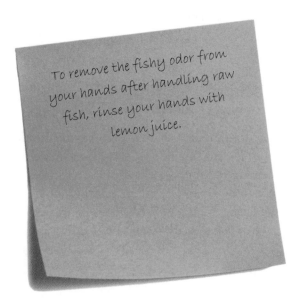

To remove the fishy odor from your hands after handling raw fish, rinse your hands with lemon juice.

Desserts & Other Sweets

Cakes • Cobblers • Pies
Cookies • Candies
Other Desserts

Chocolate Chip Cake

1 cup oil

4 eggs

1 (5.9-ounce) box instant chocolate pudding mix

1 (8-ounce) carton sour cream

1 tablespoon vanilla extract

¼ cup water

1 box butter cake mix

1 (6-ounce) package chocolate chips

Mix ingredients together; pour into greased Bundt pan. Bake at 325° for 1 hour. Cool 10 to 15 minutes in pan before serving.

Irresistible Chocolate Cake

1 box chocolate cake mix

1 (3.4-ounce) box instant chocolate pudding mix

4 large eggs, beaten

2 to 3 teaspoons instant coffee granules, dissolved in ¾ cup warm water

½ cup vegetable oil

½ cup sour cream

½ cup white chocolate chips

1 tablespoon milk

Preheat oven to 350°. Combine dry cake mix, dry pudding mix, eggs, coffee, oil and sour cream in a large bowl. Beat on high 2 minutes with an electric mixer. Pour batter into a greased 12-cup fluted tube pan. Bake 40 minutes or until toothpick inserted in cake comes out clean. Cool in pan on wire rack 10 minutes before removing to a serving platter. For glaze, combine white chocolate chips and milk in a small microwaveable bowl. Microwave 50 seconds; stir. Microwave additional 30 seconds until chips are melted. Pour warm glaze over cake. Allow to stand 30 minutes before serving.

Easiest Five Minute Cake for One

4 tablespoons cake flour (or all-purpose flour)

4 tablespoons sugar

2 tablespoons cocoa powder

1 microwaveable coffee mug

1 egg, beaten

3 tablespoons milk

3 tablespoons oil

3 tablespoons chocolate chips (optional)

1 small dash vanilla extract

Combine dry ingredients in a microwaveable mug. Add egg and mix thoroughly. Pour in milk and oil; mix well. Add chocolate chips and vanilla; mix again. Place mug in microwave and cook 3 minutes (1,000 watt microwave). Cake will rise over top of mug, but don't be alarmed. Cool 1 to 2 minutes. Tip out onto a plate or eat right out of the cup. Enjoy!

Tornado Cake

1 cup chopped pecans

1 cup coconut

1 box Swiss chocolate cake mix, plus ingredients to prepare per directions

1 (16-ounce) box powdered sugar

1 (8-ounce) package cream cheese, softened

1 stick butter, softened

Place nuts and coconut in greased 9x13-inch pan. Prepare cake batter according to directions on box; pour over pecans and coconut. Cream powdered sugar, cream cheese and butter. Spoon small dollops of butter mixture on top of cake, pushing them down into the batter. Bake at 350° for 1 hour.

Red Velvet Cake

1 box red velvet cake mix

1¼ cup milk

⅓ cup oil

3 eggs

1 (3.4-ounce) box instant vanilla pudding mix

In a large bowl, combine all ingredients until well mixed. Pour into 2 greased 9-inch cake pans. Bake at 350° for 30 to 40 minutes or until a toothpick inserted in the center comes out clean. Cool cake at least 50 minutes.

Frosting:

1 teaspoon vanilla extract

1 stick butter, softened

1 (8-ounce) package cream cheese, softened

1 (16-ounce) box powdered sugar

Mix all ingredients together. Spread on cooled cake.

The Scripture Cake

1 cup butter, softened (Judges 5:25)

2 cups sugar (Jeremiah 6:20)

3½ cups self-rising flour (1 Kings 4:22)

2 cups raisins (1 Samuel 30:12)

1 cup chopped figs (1 Samuel 30:12)

1 cup chopped almonds (Genesis 43:11)

1 cup water (Genesis 24:20)

6 eggs (Isaiah 10:14)

Pinch of salt (Exodus 16:31)

Spice to taste (1 Kings 10:2)

Mix all ingredients. Pour into greased 9x13-inch cake pan. Bake at 350° for 30 to 35 minutes or until browned on top. One word. Heavenly!

Pistachio Cake

1 box white cake mix

½ cup oil

2 (3.4-ounce) packages pistachio pudding mix

½ cup milk

½ cup water

5 eggs

Mix ingredients together and bake in treated 8-inch round cake pans at 350° for 30 minutes or until done; cool.

Icing

1 (16-ounce) box powdered sugar

1 (8-ounce) package cream cheese, softened

1 stick butter, softened

½ cup chopped pecans

Mix ingredients thoroughly and frost cake when cooled.

thinkstock / iStockphoto / Oxana Denezhkina

Classic Caramel Cake

2 sticks butter, softened

2 cups sugar

4 eggs

3 cups self-rising flour

1 cup buttermilk

2 teaspoons vanilla

Preheat oven to 350°. Grease and flour 3 9-inch cake pans. Cream butter and sugar well, beat 5 minutes or longer until mixture is light and fluffy. Add eggs, 1 at a time, mixing well after each. Add flour and buttermilk, a little at time, beginning and ending with flour, and mixing well as you add. Add vanilla and beat well. Divide better evenly between pans and bake 25 to 30 minutes, or until set. Cool 3 minutes in pan then turn unto cooling racks to cool completely.

Caramel Frosting

2 cups sugar

1 cup buttermilk

½ cup Crisco

½ cup butter

1 teaspoon baking soda

Combine all ingredients in a large saucepan. Stirring continuously, cook to softball stage (235° to 245°) on a candy thermometer or when tested in a cup of cold water. Remove from heat and beat with a wooden spoon until creamy and ready to spread.

Butternut Cake

1¼ cup Crisco

6 eggs

2 cups sugar

¼ teaspoon salt

3 teaspoons vanilla butternut flavoring

½ cup evaporated milk

2 cups all-purpose flour

1 teaspoon baking powder

Preheat oven to 325°. Combine Crisco, eggs, sugar, salt and butter nut vanilla flavoring until light and fluffy. Add milk and mix well. Sift flour and baking powder and add to batter; mix well on high speed. Bake in 2 8-inch layers 40 minutes or until a toothpick inserted in the center comes out clean. Cool cakes completely on a wire rack. When cool, frost between layers and outside of cake with Butternut Frosting.

Butternut Frosting

1 stick butter

1 (8-ounce) package cream cheese

1 teaspoon vanilla butternut flavoring

1 (16-ounce) box powdered sugar

2 cups finely chopped pecans

Mix butter, cream cheese and flavoring until fluffy. Add powdered sugar 1 cup at a time, blending on high speed in between each addition. Add pecans and mix well.

This recipe can be made as pound cake by baking 40 minutes in a tube pan. Cover the top with Butternut Frosting. You can freeze the left-over frosting and have enough for two more cakes.

1-2-3-4 Cake

1 cup shortening

2 cups sugar

3 cups flour

4 eggs, beaten

1¼ cups milk

1 teaspoon vanilla extract

Icing, your choice

Cream together shortening, sugar, flour, eggs, milk and vanilla. Pour into 3 round, greased cake pans. Bake at 350° for 30 minutes. Frost with icing when cool.

Whipping Cream Pound Cake

3 cups sugar

1 cup butter, softened

6 eggs

3 cups self-rising flour

1 teaspoon almond extract

1 cup whipping cream

Cream sugar and butter; stir in remaining ingredients. Mix well. Grease and flour a tube pan. Pour in batter. Put in cold oven. Set oven on to 325° and bake 1 hour and 25 minutes. Cool 5 minutes then remove from pan.

Sour Cream Pound Cake

1 box butter cake mix

½ cup sugar

¾ cup oil

1 (8-ounce) carton sour cream

4 eggs

Mix all ingredients. Bake in a greased Bundt pan at
350° for 50 minutes to 1 hour.

Granny's Vanilla Wafer Cake

2 sticks butter, softened

2 cups sugar

6 eggs, beaten

1 (12-ounce) box vanilla wafers, crushed

½ cup milk

1 teaspoon vanilla extract

1 (7-ounce) package coconut

1 cup chopped pecans

Cream butter and sugar; stir in eggs. Mix well. Add crushed
wafers alternately with milk. Mix in vanilla, coconut and
pecans. Pour into greased and floured Bundt pan and bake at
325° for 1 hour and 15 minutes.

Moist Bundt Cake

1 box yellow cake mix

4 eggs, beaten

1 cup Sprite

¾ cup oil

1 (14½-ounce) can coconut pecan frosting

1 cup chopped pecans

Combine dry cake mix, eggs, Sprite and oil until well blended. Stir in frosting and nuts. Pour into greased Bundt cake pan and bake at 350° for 1 hour.

To double your frosting for cakes and cupcakes, whip store-bought frosting with a mixer for a few minutes or until it doubles in size. Not only will you be able to frost more desserts, you will end up eating less sugar, fat and calories per serving.

Coconut & Sour Cream Cake

1 box butter cake mix, plus ingredients to prepare per directions

1 cup sour cream

2 (8-ounce) packages frozen coconut, defrosted

¾ cup sugar

Bake cake according to package directions in a 9x13-inch pan. Mix sour cream, coconut and sugar together in a bowl. While cake is still hot, use a knife to slit holes in the top. Spread coconut mixture over cake.

Fruit Cocktail Cake

1 box yellow cake mix

1 (16-ounce) can fruit cocktail

2 eggs

1 stick butter

1 cup sugar

1 teaspoon vanilla extract

1 cup evaporated milk

1 cup chopped nuts

1 cup coconut

Combine dry cake mix, fruit cocktail and eggs. Beat with mixer until fruit is broken into bits. Pour batter into greased and floured 9x13-inch baking pan. Bake at 350° for 40 minutes. About 15 minutes before cake is done, melt butter with sugar in a saucepan over medium-low heat; cook 10 minutes. Stir in vanilla, milk, nuts and coconut. Poke holes in top of cake with a fork. Pour icing over warm cake.

Cajun Cake

¼ cup oil

2 eggs, beaten

1 (15.25-ounce) can crushed pineapple

1 box butter cake mix

Preheat oven to 350°. Pour oil in 9x13-inch baking pan. Mix remaining ingredients. Beat 2 minutes. Pour into prepared pan. Bake 35 minutes.

Icing:

1 stick butter

⅔ cup evaporated milk

1 cup sugar

1 cup chopped pecans

1 cup coconut

In a saucepan, combine butter, milk and sugar. Bring to a boil, stirring frequently. Boil 2 minutes, stirring constantly. Remove from heat. Add nuts and coconut; spread over warm cake.

Coconut Pineapple Cake

1 box yellow cake mix, plus ingredients to prepare per directions

1 (20-ounce) can crushed pineapple

1 cup sugar

1 large (4.6-ounce) box cook & serve vanilla pudding mix (not instant), plus ingredients to prepare per directions

1 cup whipping cream, whipped

1 cup chopped pecans

Shredded coconut

Prepare cake according to package directions. Bake in a 9x13-inch baking dish. In a medium saucepan, cook pineapple with its juice and sugar, stirring frequently, until sugar dissolves. Remove from heat. Prepare pudding as directed on package. After baking, poke holes in top of cake with a straw. Pour pineapple mixture over cake. Pour pudding over pineapple mixture. Spread whipped cream over top. Sprinkle pecans then coconut over whipped cream. Chill at least 24 hours before serving

Aunt Kristy's Best Coconut Cake

1 box white cake mix, plus ingredients to prepare per directions

1 (15-ounce) can cream of coconut

1 (14-ounce) can sweetened condensed milk

1 (8-ounce) carton whipped topping

1 (7-ounce) bag coconut

Bake cake in a 9x13-inch baking dish according to package directions. Cool. Poke holes in top of cake with a straw. Pour cream of coconut and then condensed milk over cake. Top with whipped topping. Sprinkle coconut over top. Refrigerate 2 hours or until ready to serve.

My aunt Kristy Lepard says this cake is great any time of year, but it makes a great holiday cake. At Christmas, she decorates it with peppermint candies or cherries.

What do you do with all that left-over hard candy and candy canes after the holidays? Try chopping the candy and adding it to your brownie and cake batters before baking. Or, stir it into hot coffee and cocoa, and let it melt before drinking. Sprinkle over ice cream or frosted cakes. You can even add the chopped candy to preserves for a minty treat.

Granny's 7-Up Cake

1 box yellow cake mix

1 (3.4-ounce) box instant vanilla pudding

4 eggs, beaten

10 ounces 7-Up (lemon-lime soft drink)

Combine all ingredients. Pour into greased 9x13-inch pan. Bake at 350° for 25 to 30 minutes. Cool before frosting.

Frosting

1 (13-ounce) can crushed pineapple, drained

1 stick butter

2 tablespoons flour

1½ cups sugar

2 eggs

1¼ cups flaked coconut

Combine pineapple, butter, flour, sugar and eggs. Cook over medium heat until thick. Remove from heat; cool. Stir in coconut and spread over cake.

Cakes

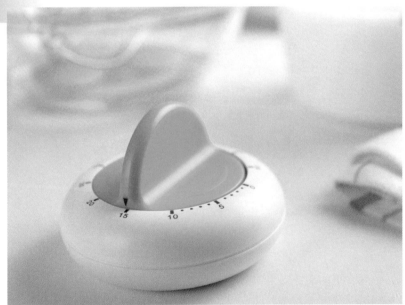

thinkstock / iStockphoto / Lilyana Vynogradova

Elvis Presley Cake

1 box butter cake mix, plus ingredients to prepare per directions

2 cups sugar

1 (15½-ounce) can crushed pineapple (with juice)

1¼ cups flaked coconut

Bake cake as directed in a 9x13-inch pan. In a saucepan, cook sugar, pineapple, and coconut over medium heat 10 minutes. Poke holes in top of cake with a straw. Spread mixture over warm cake.

Icing

1 stick butter, softened

1 (8-ounce) package cream cheese, softened

1 (16-ounce) box powdered sugar

1 teaspoon vanilla extract

Cream butter and cream cheese; add sugar and mix well. Mix in vanilla and spread over cake.

Mountain High Cake

1 box yellow cake mix

1 (3-ounce) box Jell-O Cook & Serve Coconut Cream Pudding

1 (12-ounce) can Mountain Dew

4 eggs, beaten

1 cup oil

Combine dry cake mix and dry pudding mix. Add remaining ingredients and mix well. Bake in a greased 9x13-inch pan at 350° for 40 minutes.

Topping

1 cup sugar

4 tablespoons flour

1 (16-ounce) can crushed pineapple (with juice)

1¼ cups flaked coconut

Combine all ingredients except coconut in a saucepan. Cook, stirring until thick and clear. Remove from heat; cool. Stir in coconut. Spread over cake.

Pineapple Sheet Cake

2 cups flour

1½ cups sugar

1 teaspoon baking soda

1 (8-ounce) can crushed pineapple

2 eggs, beaten

½ cup brown sugar

½ cup chopped pecans

Mix flour, sugar, baking soda, pineapple (with juice) and eggs; stir well. Pour into a greased 9x13-inch pan. Mix brown sugar and nuts; sprinkle over batter. Bake at 350° for 30 minutes.

Icing

1 cup evaporated milk

¾ cup sugar

1 stick butter

In a saucepan, bring evaporated milk, sugar and butter to a boil over medium-high heat. Boil 3 minutes, stirring almost constantly. Cool to warm, but not hot. Spread on cake before cake cools.

When I was about 10 years old, my grandma "Marene" (said Mah-reen-ee) took me to a Halloween carnival where we played musical chairs and I won a Carrot Cake. Ever since then, Carrot Cake is one of my favorite desserts, and this recipe is simply delicious.

Carrot Cake

3 cups grated carrots

2 cups each flour and sugar

1 teaspoon cinnamon

4 eggs

1½ cups oil

1¼ teaspoons vanilla extract

1 (8-ounce) can crushed pineapple with juice

¾ cup chopped pecans

Icing

3½ cups powdered sugar

1 (8-ounce) package cream cheese, softened

1 stick butter, softened

1¼ teaspoons vanilla extract

1 cup chopped pecans

Mix all ingredients together. Pour into a greased 9x13-inch pan and bake at 350° for 40 to 45 minutes. Cool. Beat icing ingredients, except pecans, until smooth. Stir in pecans. Spread over cake.

thinkstock / iStockphoto / Yelena Yemchuk

Orange Pound Cake

1 box orange cake mix

4 eggs, beaten

1 (3.4-ounce) package instant vanilla pudding

1 (11-ounce) can mandarin oranges, drained

½ cup oil

Combine all ingredients and pour into a greased Bundt pan. Bake at 350° for 35 to 40 minutes or until a toothpick pressed into the center comes out clean.

Everyone's Favorite Mandarin Orange Cake

1 box yellow cake mix

1 (11-ounce) can mandarin oranges with juice

½ cup vegetable oil

3 eggs

Frosting

1 (8-ounce) container whipped topping

1 (8-ounce) can crushed pineapple

1 (3.4-ounce) box instant vanilla pudding mix

Grease and lightly flour 2 round layer cake pans. Combine all ingredients and mix well. Pour into prepared pans. Bake at 350° until lightly browned on top, about 25 minutes. After cake has cooled completely, combine frosting ingredients and frost cake.

This recipe is very special to me because it was my Granny Bobbie's favorite dessert.

Strawberry Cake

1 box white cake mix

4 eggs, beaten

½ cup oil

1 (3-ounce) box strawberry Jell-O

1 (8-ounce) package frozen sliced strawberries with juice, thawed

Combine all ingredients in mixing bowl; beat with mixer 3 minutes. Pour into a greased 9x13-inch pan. Bake at 350° for 50 minutes. Cool before frosting.

Frosting

1 (8-ounce) package frozen sliced strawberries, thawed and well-drained (save juice)

1 (16-ounce) box powdered sugar

½ stick butter, softened

Combine all ingredients except reserved juice. Gradually mix in strawberry juice to spreadable consistency.

thinkstock / iStockphoto / Teresa Kasprzycka

Lemon Cake

**1 box yellow cake mix,
plus ingredients to prepare per directions**

**1 (3.4-ounce) package instant lemon Jell-O,
plus ingredients to prepare per directions**

1 (14-ounce) can sweetened condensed milk

1 (8-ounce) carton whipped topping

½ cup lemon juice

Mix cake as directed and bake in a treated 9x13-inch pan; cool. Prepare Jell-O as directed, but do not chill. Punch holes in top of cake with a straw. Pour Jell-O over cake. Combine milk, whipped topping and lemon juice; spread over cake. Refrigerate until ready to serve.

Lemon Icebox Cake

**1 box butter cake mix,
plus ingredients to prepare per directions**

2 (14-ounce) cans sweetened condensed milk

½ cup lemon juice

1 (12-ounce) container whipped topping

Prepare cake mix as directed on package. Pour batter into 3 greased 9-inch round cake pans. Bake as directed; cool. After cake has cooled, combine condensed milk and lemon juice until well blended. Place 1 layer on a serving platter; coat top with lemon milk. Place second layer over first and coat top with lemon milk. Top with third layer. Mix whipped topping into remaining lemon milk and frost cake.

Blueberry Cake

1 box butter cake mix

½ cup sugar

1 stick butter, melted

3 eggs

1 (8-ounce) package cream cheese, softened

1 cup blueberries

½ cup chopped pecans

Preheat oven to 350°. Mix all ingredients together except berries and pecans. Gently stir in berries and nuts until fully mixed. Pour into greased Bundt pan and bake 35 minutes.

thinkstock / iStockphoto / Kati Molin

Cakes

Blueberry Pound Cake

1 box butter cake mix

1 (8-ounce) package cream cheese, softened

½ cup oil

3 eggs, beaten

2 cups blueberries

Combine all ingredients except blueberries. Beat until smooth. Fold in blueberries. Bake in a greased and floured Bundt pan at 325° for 1 hour or until done.

Indian Quick Cake

1 (15.25-ounce) can sliced peaches, drained (juice reserved)

1 box butter cake mix

1 stick butter plus more for greasing pan

Grease a 9x13-inch pan with butter. Arrange drained peaches in pan. Sprinkle dry cake mix evenly over top; do not stir. Pour reserved peach juice over cake mix. Top with dabs of butter. Bake at 350° for 1 hour.

Peach Cobbler

½ stick (4 tablespoons) butter

1 (15-ounce) can sliced peaches

⅔ cup flour

⅔ cup sugar

⅔ cup milk

Preheat oven to 350°. Melt butter in 8-inch square baking dish. Pour peaches with juice over butter. In a separate bowl, mix flour, sugar and milk together; pour over peaches. Bake 45 minutes.

thinkstock / iStockphoto / Charles Brutlag

Pear Cobbler

2 (16-ounce) can sliced pears, drained

1 box yellow cake mix

½ cup sugar

3 teaspoons cinnamon

2 sticks butter

½ cup chopped nuts

Arrange pears in a 9x13-inch baking dish. Pour dry cake mix over pears. Mix sugar and cinnamon and sprinkle over cake mix. Slice butter into tablespoon-size pieces and place on top of mixture. Sprinkle nuts on top. Bake at 325° for 35 to 40 minutes.

Deep-Dish Plum Cobbler

2½ pounds plums, pitted and sliced

1½ cups sugar

¼ cup quick-cooking tapioca

¼ teaspoon almond extract

⅛ teaspoon salt

2 tablespoons cold butter

Pastry for 1 (9-inch) pie crust

1 egg white

Place plums in a large bowl. In another bowl, combine sugar, tapioca, almond extract and salt. Cut in butter until crumbly; gently stir into plums. Let stand 15 minutes. Transfer to a greased 2½-quart baking dish. Roll out pastry to ⅛-inch thickness. Cut into strips and make a lattice over filling. Trim edges. Beat egg white until foamy; brush over pastry. Bake at 425° for 40 to 45 minutes or until golden brown.

Apple Cobbler

1 stick butter

2 cups sugar

2 cups water

½ cup shortening

1½ cups sifted self-rising flour

⅓ cup milk

1 teaspoon cinnamon

2 cups finely chopped apples

Preheat oven to 350°. Melt butter in a 9x13-inch pan. In a saucepan, heat sugar and water until sugar melts then remove from heat. Cut shortening into flour. Add milk and stir with a fork until dough leaves sides of bowl. Knead on floured surface until smooth. Roll dough into a large rectangle about ¼-inch thick. Sprinkle cinnamon over apples. Spread apples evenly across dough. Roll-up dough like a jelly roll. Dampen edge with a little water to seal. Slice dough in ½-inch thick slices and place in prepared pan cut side down. Pour sugar water around slices. Bake 55 minutes to 1 hour.

Apple Stuff

11 apples

1 (6-ounce) package strawberry flavored gelatin

½ cup butter, softened

1 cup all-purpose flour

1 cup sugar

Preheat oven to 350°. Peel, core and chop apples. Spread them in a 9x13-inch baking dish. Cover apples with gelatin. Mix together the butter, flour and sugar until well combined. Sprinkle over the apples. Bake at 350° for 45 minutes.

Blackberry Cobbler

2 cups blackberries

½ cup water

1½ cups sugar, divided use

1 stick butter, melted

1 cup flour

1 cup milk

In a saucepan, mix berries, water and ½ cup sugar. Bring to a boil then reduce heat to medium and let simmer while preparing batter. Pour melted butter into bottom of 9x9-inch square baking dish. In separate bowl mix flour, 1 cup sugar and milk. Pour over butter; do not stir. Pour blackberries over batter; do not stir. Bake at 350° for 1 hour.

thinkstock / iStockphoto / Stephanie Frey

Blueberry Crumble

**2 (18- to 20-ounce) packages blueberry muffin mix,
plus ingredients to prepare muffins**

1 cup quick oats

½ cup sugar

1 teaspoon cinnamon

1 stick butter, melted

Mix blueberry mixes according to package directions. Spread in a 9x13-inch pan. Mix oats, sugar and cinnamon. Sprinkle over batter. Pour melted butter over batter. Bake at 375° until golden brown, about 12 to 15 minutes.

Cherry Cobbler

1 (15-ounce) can tart red cherries

1 cup all-purpose flour

1¼ cups sugar, divided use

1 cup milk

2 teaspoons baking powder

⅛ teaspoon salt

½ cup butter, melted

Whipped topping (optional)

In a saucepan over medium heat, cook cherries with their juice until boiling; remove from heat. In a medium bowl, mix flour, 1 cup sugar, milk, baking powder and salt. Pour butter into a 2-quart casserole dish or 4 to 6 1-cup ramekins; spoon flour mixture over butter. Add cherries; do not stir. Sprinkle remaining ¼ cup sugar over top. Bake at 400° for 20 to 30 minutes. Serve warm, with whipped topping if desired. Makes 4 to 6 servings.

Cherry Fluff Pie

1 (15.25-ounce) can crushed pineapple, drained

1 (21-ounce) can cherry pie filling

1 cup flaked coconut

1 cup chopped pecans

1 (16-ounce) carton whipped topping

1 (14-ounce) can sweetened condensed milk

1 graham cracker crust

Mix all filling ingredients together. Pour into pie crust. Chill overnight. You can chop pecans easier use a food chopper or try closing them in a zip-lock bag and crushing them with a rolling pin or a metal spatula.

Chocolate-Cherry Pie

1 (12-ounce) package semisweet chocolate morsels

1 (14-ounce) can sweetened condensed milk

1 (20-ounce) can cherry pie filling

1 graham cracker crust

1 (8-ounce) carton whipped topping

Combine chocolate morsels and milk in a large microwave-safe bowl. Microwave until morsels are melted; stir well. Mix in cherry pie filling, stirring until well combined. Pour into pie crust. Top with whipped topping. Chill before serving.

Pies

Butterfinger Pie

4 (2.1-ounce) Butterfinger candy bars, crushed (reserve ¼ cup)

1 (8-ounce) package cream cheese, softened

1 (8-ounce) container whipped topping

1 graham cracker crust

With an electric mixer, combine all filling ingredients (except reserved Butterfingers). Pour into pie crust. Top with reserved candy. Chill overnight before serving.

My good friend Diane says, "This is the favorite dessert of my son, Trey, and daughter, Ashley. Even though both are grown, they still love it when mama makes it for her babies."

Peanut Butter Pie

1 (8-ounce) package cream cheese, softened

1 cup powdered sugar

1 cup peanut butter

1 (8-ounce) carton whipped topping

1 graham cracker crust

Blend all filling ingredients together until smooth. Pour into pie crust and chill.

Ice Cream Pie

1 (16-ounce) package Oreo cookies

1 stick butter, melted

1 quart vanilla ice cream, softened

1 pint chocolate ice cream, softened

1 (8-ounce) carton whipped topping

Chopped walnuts

Chocolate syrup

Crush cookies; mix with butter and press into a 9-inch deep-dish pie plate to form the crust. Layer vanilla ice cream over crust. Top with chocolate ice cream. Freeze 2 hours or until ready to serve. Before serving, thaw 5 minutes. Top with whipped topping and nuts. Drizzle chocolate over top.

Pies

Hawaiian Delight

1 (14-ounce) can sweetened condensed milk

12 tablespoons lemon juice

1 (8-ounce) container whipped topping

1 (8-ounce) can crushed pineapple, drained

1 cup chopped pecans

1 graham cracker pie crust

Mix ingredients together and pour into pie crust. Let stand in refrigerator 30 minutes before serving.

Heavenly Pie

1 (14-ounce) can sweetened condensed milk

1 cup graham cracker crumbs

½ stick butter, melted

2 or 3 bananas

4 ounces whipped topping

Chopped pecans, as many as you wish

To make caramel, place condensed milk (in the unopened can; wrapper removed) in a large pot. Add water to cover by 2 inches. Bring to rolling boil and continue to boil 2½ hours. (Very Important; The can must remain completely submerged the entire process; add more water as needed.) Cool before opening can. Mix cracker crumbs and butter and press into bottom of an 8-inch pie plate. Arrange sliced bananas over crust. Sprinkle with pecans and top with caramel. Sprinkle with more pecans and top with whipped topping. Top with additional pecans, if desired.

Lemonade Pie

1 (6-ounce) can lemonade concentrate, partially thawed

1 (14-ounce) can sweetened condensed milk

1 (8-ounce) container whipped topping

1 graham cracker crust

Combine lemonade concentrate with milk. Fold in whipped topping. Pour into pie shell. Chill.

Key Lime Pie

½ cup lime juice

1 (14 ounce) can sweetened condensed milk

1 (8-ounce) pack cream cheese, softened

1 graham cracker crust

1 (8-ounce) container whipped topping

Combine lime juice, sweetened condensed milk, and cream cheese; beat with mixer until smooth and thick. Pour into pie crust. Cover and chill 1 hour or until ready to serve. Top with whipped topping before serving.

Million Dollar Pie

1 (14-ounce) can sweetened condensed milk

1 (8-ounce) container whipped topping

1 (15.25-ounce) can crushed pineapple, drained

⅓ cup lemon juice

1 cup chopped pecans

1¼ cups flaked coconut

2 graham cracker crusts

Mix all ingredients together. Pour into pie crusts and chill in refrigerator.

thinkstock / iStockphoto / Yelena Yemchuk

Say Cheese Pear Pie

4 large ripe pears, peeled and thinly sliced

⅓ cup sugar

1 tablespoon cornstarch

⅛ teaspoon salt

1 (9-inch) unbaked pie shell

Cheese Topping

½ cup shredded Cheddar cheese

½ cup all-purpose flour

¼ cup sugar

¼ teaspoon salt

¼ cup butter, melted

Combine pears, sugar, cornstarch and salt; toss gently to coat pears. Pour into pie shell. Combine Cheese Topping ingredients and sprinkle over filling. Bake at 425° for 25 to 35 minutes or until crust is golden brown and cheese is melted. Cool before cutting; refrigerate left-overs.

Strawberry Cheesecake

2 (8-ounce) packages cream cheese, softened

3 eggs, beaten

¾ cup sugar

½ tablespoon vanilla extract

1 graham cracker crust

1 (21-ounce) can strawberry pie filling

In a large bowl, combine cream cheese, eggs, sugar and vanilla; beat well with a mixer. Preheat oven to 325°. Pour mixture into the pie crust. Bake for 25 minutes. Remove from oven and chill. Top with strawberry pie filling. Chill before serving.

Fresh Strawberry Pie

1 cup sugar

4 tablespoons flour

1 (12-ounce) can 7-Up

1 pint fresh strawberries, sliced

1 (8-inch) pie shell, baked and cooled

1 (8-ounce) carton whipped topping

In a saucepan, mix sugar, flour and 7-Up. Cook over medium heat, stirring until thick. Let cool. Add strawberries. Pour into pie shell and cover with whipped topping. Refrigerate 1 hour or until ready to serve.

Chocolate Pie

2 cups milk, scalded

5 large egg yolks

4 tablespoons cocoa powder

1 cup sugar

5 tablespoons cornstarch

4 tablespoons margarine

1 teaspoon vanilla extract

1 (9-inch) pie shell, baked

Preheat oven to 350°. While crust is baking, combine scalded milk, cocoa, sugar, cornstarch, margarine and vanilla in the top of a double boiler. Mix well. Stir in egg yolks; mix well. Cook over boiling water until thick. Pour into pie shell. Top with meringue and bake just until meringue is lightly browned, about 10 minutes.

Meringue

5 large egg whites

1 teaspoon vanilla extract

½ cup sugar

Beat egg whites with vanilla until soft peaks form. Gradually add sugar while beating on high until sugar dissolves and stiff peaks form. Spread on pie.

Raisin Pie

⅓ cup butter, softened

1 cup sugar

2 eggs, separated

¼ cup milk

½ cup chopped walnuts

1 cup raisins

1 unbaked pie pastry (9 inches)

Whipped topping, optional

Cream butter and sugar with an electric mixer. Add egg yolks; beat well. Blend in milk. With a spoon, gently stir in nuts and raisins; set aside. Using clean beaters, beat egg whites until stiff peaks form; fold into raisin mixture. Pour into pie shell. Bake at 350° for 15 minutes. Reduce oven temperature to 300°; bake 40 minutes longer or until lightly browned. Cool. Refrigerate until ready to serve, at least 1 hour. Top with whipped topping before serving, if desired.

Green Tomato Pie

1½ cups sugar

5 tablespoons all-purpose flour

1 teaspoon ground cinnamon

Pinch salt

4 or 5 medium green tomatoes (3 cups thinly sliced)

1 tablespoon cider vinegar

Pastry for double-crust (9-inch) pie

1 tablespoon butter

Combine sugar, flour, cinnamon and salt. Add tomatoes and vinegar; toss to coat. Line a 9-inch pie plate with bottom crust. Add filling; dot with butter. Roll out remaining pastry; make a lattice crust. Trim, seal and flute edges. Bake at 350° for 1 hour or until tomatoes are tender. Cool on a wire rack to room temperature. Refrigerate until ready to serve and refrigerate left-overs.

Sand Tarts

2 sticks butter, softened

4 tablespoons sugar

2½ cups all-purpose flour

1 teaspoon vanilla extract

1 cup chopped pecans

Powdered sugar

Cream butter and slowly add sugar. Stir in flour.
Add vanilla and pecans. Shape into crescents on
a large cookie sheet. Bake at 250° for 45 minutes.
Roll in powdered sugar when cool.

thinkstock / iStockphoto / AnjelaGr

Sugar Cookies

2 cups self-rising flour

1½ cups sugar, plus more for tops

1 egg

1 teaspoon vanilla extract

1 cup oil

Mix all ingredients together. Roll dough into balls and place on ungreased cookie sheet. Bake at 350° until edges are brown, about 10 minutes. While still warm, sprinkle cookies with sugar.

bigstockphoto / Ollzha

Tea Cakes

2 cups self-rising flour

1 cup sugar

½ cup oil

2 eggs, beaten

1 teaspoon vanilla extract

Spray cookie sheet with nonstick spray. Mix all ingredients; roll into balls with moist hands. Put on cookie sheet 2 to 3 inches apart. Bake at 375° for 10 to 15 minutes.

Butter Cookies

1 box butter cake mix

1 stick butter, melted

2 eggs

Mix all ingredients together. Drop by spoonfuls onto greased cookie sheet. Bake at 350° for 8 to 10 minutes.

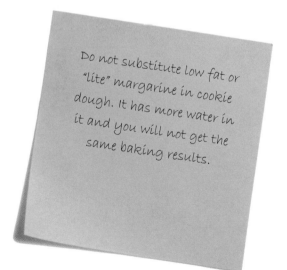

Do not substitute low fat or "lite" margarine in cookie dough. It has more water in it and you will not get the same baking results.

Cookies

Easy Peanut Butter Cookies

1 cup peanut butter

1 egg

1 cup sugar

1 teaspoon vanilla extract

Mix ingredients together. Roll into balls. Place on cookie
sheet and flatten. Bake at 350° for 10 minutes.

thinkstock / istockphoto / Margaret Edwards

Just Easy Cookies

1 box cake mix, any flavor

1 (8-ounce) carton whipped topping

1 egg

Powdered sugar

Mix all ingredients except powdered sugar. Roll dough into balls, then roll in powdered sugar. Do not flatten. Bake at 350° for 12 minutes. Let cool.

Monster Cookies

12 eggs

2 pounds brown sugar

4 cups sugar

1 tablespoon vanilla extract

1 tablespoon dark corn syrup

8 teaspoons baking soda

1 pound butter

1 (3-pound) jar peanut butter

18 cups quick oats

1 pound chocolate chips

1 pound M&M's

Thoroughly mix all ingredients together. Using an ice cream scoop, drop scoops of dough onto greased cookie sheets, 6 per sheet. Flatten cookies. Bake at 350° for 12 minutes. Do not over-bake.

Pecan Butter Balls

1 cup butter, softened

¼ cup sugar

1 tablespoon vanilla extract

2 cups all-purpose flour, sifted

2 cups finely chopped pecans

Powdered sugar

Cream butter and sugar; add vanilla. Stir in flour and pecans. Roll into small balls; place on greased cookie sheets. Bake at 325° for 25 minutes. While hot, roll in powdered sugar.

Pecan Pie Cookies

1 stick butter, softened

1 cup firmly packed dark brown sugar

1 egg

1 cup all-purpose flour

1 cup chopped pecans

Mix all ingredients together; spoon onto ungreased cookie sheets. Bake in 375° oven 12 to 15 minutes. Allow to cool 2 minutes on sheets, then move to wire rack to cool completely.

Let cookie dough "rest" or chill in refrigerator before forming if you want uniform cookies that don't flatten out and get too brown around the edges.

Cookies

Chocolate Chip Cookies

½ cup butter

½ cup sugar

½ cup brown sugar

1⅛ cups flour

½ teaspoon baking soda

½ teaspoon salt

1 egg, lightly beaten

1 teaspoon vanilla extract

½ (12-ounce) bag chocolate chips

Melt butter in a small pan. Add both sugars; stir. Let cool. Mix flour, baking soda and salt together. Add egg and vanilla to butter mixture. Stir in chocolate chips. Refrigerate dough about an hour. Drop by teaspoons onto greased cookie sheet. Bake at 375° for 10 minutes.

thinkstock / istockphoto / KEMAL BAÃ...Âž

Oatmeal Cookies

1¼ cups sugar

½ cup shortening

2 eggs

1½ cups quick oats

½ cup buttermilk

1½ cups sifted flour

1½ teaspoons baking powder

1½ teaspoons baking soda

¾ teaspoon salt

¾ teaspoon cinnamon

¾ teaspoon nutmeg

¾ teaspoon ground cloves

¾ cup raisins

Cream sugar, shortening and eggs; add oats and buttermilk; mix well. Combine flour, baking powder, soda, salt and spices; stir into oat mixture. Add raisins. Drop from teaspoon 2 inches apart on greased cookie sheet. Bake at 375° for 12 to 15 minutes.

Carrot Cookies

1 cup sugar

¾ cup butter

1 egg

1 cup mashed, cooked carrots

2 cups flour

2½ teaspoons baking powder

Cream sugar, butter, egg and carrots. Sift dry ingredients together. Gradually stir into creamed mixture. Drop by spoonfuls onto greased cookie sheet. Bake at 350° for 12 to 15 minutes.

Coconut Fruitcake Cookies

3 cups chopped pecans

2½ cups flaked coconut

1¼ cups chopped candied cherries

1¼ cups chopped candied pineapple

1 cup chopped dates

2 cups sweetened condensed milk

In a bowl, combine the first 5 ingredients. Stir in milk. Fill paper-lined miniature muffin cups two-thirds full. Bake at 300° for 20 to 25 minutes or until golden brown. Cool 10 minutes before removing to wax paper to cool completely. Let stand 24 hours in airtight container at room temperature before serving.

Lemon Cookies

1 envelope Dream Whip mix

½ cup milk

1 box lemon cake mix

1 egg

Powdered sugar

Preheat oven to 350°. Combine Dream Whip and milk. Add cake mix and egg; blend well. Roll dough into 1-inch balls. Dip balls in powdered sugar. Spray cookie sheet with nonstick spray. Place cookies 2 inches apart on cookie sheet (do not flatten). Bake 8 minutes. Do not let cookies brown. They should be extra moist.

Gingerbread Cookies

1 cup shortening

1 cup sugar

½ teaspoon salt

1 egg

1 cup molasses

2 tablespoons white vinegar

5 cups sifted all-purpose flour

1½ teaspoons baking soda

1 tablespoon ginger

1 teaspoon cinnamon

1 teaspoon ground cloves

Red hots

Cream shortening, sugar and salt; stir in egg, molasses and vinegar; beat well. Combine dry ingredients; stir into molasses mixture. Chill about 3 hours; roll ⅛-inch thick on lightly floured surface. Cut with gingerbread cutter. Place 1 inch apart on greased cookie sheet. Use red hots for faces and buttons. Bake 6 minutes at 375°. Cool slightly and decorate with icing.

Icing

1¼ cups powdered sugar

3 tablespoons milk

½ teaspoon clear vanilla extract

Stir milk and vanilla into powdered sugar and mix well.

Cookies

Macaroons

2 (8-ounce) packages shredded coconut

2 teaspoons vanilla extract

1 (14-ounce) can sweetened condensed milk

Mix all ingredients until well blended. Drop teaspoonfuls onto well-greased cookie sheet. Bake at 350° for 10 to 12 minutes. Cool 1 minute before moving to wire rack.

Almond Bark Drop Cookies

2 pounds white confectionery coating (white almond bark)

1 cup peanut butter

2 cups dry-roasted peanuts

3 cups crisp rice cereal

2 cups miniature marshmallows

In a microwave oven or over a double boiler, melt the white confectionery coating, stirring frequently until smooth. Remove from heat. Stir in peanut butter until well blended. Fold in the peanuts, rice cereal and marshmallows. Drop by heaping spoonfuls onto wax paper-lined baking sheets. Chill until set; store in refrigerator.

Cookies

Pistachio Balls

3 tablespoons baking cocoa

1 (14-ounce) can sweetened condensed milk

2 tablespoons butter

1 cup shelled pistachios, finely chopped

Bring cocoa, milk and butter to a boil, stirring constantly. Reduce heat to low; cook and stir until thickened. Pour into a small bowl. Cover and refrigerate until chilled. Roll into 1-inch balls; roll in pistachios.

No Bake Chocolate Cookies

1 stick margarine

2 cups sugar

4 tablespoons cocoa powder

½ cup milk

Pinch salt

1 teaspoon vanilla extract

3 cups oats

1 cup chopped pecans

Combine first 5 ingredients in a saucepan and boil 2 minutes. Remove from stove. Add remaining ingredients and mix well. Drop by teaspoons onto wax paper. Let cool.

Orange Balls

1 (12-ounce) package vanilla wafers, crushed

1 stick margarine, softened

1 (12-ounce) can frozen orange juice, defrosted

1 (16-ounce) box powdered sugar

1 cup chopped nuts

Shredded coconut

Mix all ingredients except coconut. Chill dough. Roll into small balls, then roll in coconut. No baking necessary; ready to eat. Refrigerate leftovers.

thinkstock / istockphoto / Michael Gray

Cookies

Cookie Balls

1 (16-ounce) package Oreos

1 (8-ounce) package cream cheese, softened

1 (24-ounce) package vanilla almond bark

Lollipop sticks (optional)

Crush cookies. Mix in cream cheese. Form into balls. Melt white chocolate and dip each ball into chocolate to coat. Place on wax paper to set up and harden. For dipping and serving, insert lollipop sticks into balls and make Lollipop Cookie Balls.

thinkstock / istockphoto / Catherine Murray

Mint Chocolate Cookies

¾ cup butter

1½ cups brown sugar

2 tablespoons water

1 (12-ounce) package semi-sweet chocolate chips

2 eggs, beaten

2½ cups flour

1¼ teaspoon baking soda

½ teaspoon salt

Heat butter, brown sugar, water and chocolate chips in a small saucepan until chocolate chips are melted; cool slightly. In a separate bowl, combine eggs, flour, baking soda and salt. Stir in chocolate mixture until mixed well. Shape rounded tablespoons into balls and place on a cookie sheet. Lightly press each ball to flatten. Bake at 350 for 9 to 11 minutes. Remove from oven and immediately place an Andes Mint on top of each cookie. When melted, smooth mint chocolate over cookie. Cool completely before serving.

Tory's Seven Layer Cookies

5 tablespoons butter or margarine

1½ cups graham cracker crumbs

1 cup flaked coconut

1 cup semisweet chocolate chips

1 cup butterscotch chips

1 cup chopped nuts

1 (14-ounce) can sweetened condensed milk

Put butter in 9-inch square pan in 325° oven. When butter is melted, spread graham cracker crumbs evenly over the butter. Top crumbs with the coconut, then chocolate chips, butterscotch chips, and finally the nuts. Do not mix layers! Pour condensed milk over the top and bake at 325° about 30 minutes (25 minutes if you are using a glass dish). Cut into 1½-inch squares.

Short Bread Squares

1 cup butter, softened

2 cups all-purpose flour

½ cup powdered sugar

Dash salt

Preheat oven to 325°. Cream butter; add flour and sugar and mix into soft dough. Press into a 9-inch square pan; bake 20 to 25 minutes. Cut into squares before shortbread cools.

Easy Graham Cracker Squares

32 crushed graham crackers

1 (12-ounce) package semi-sweet chocolate chips

1 (14-ounce) can sweetened condensed milk

1 teaspoon vanilla

Dash salt

Mix all ingredients. Spread on a 10½x15-inch cookie sheet. Bake at 350° for 15 minutes. Cool and cut into squares.

Cookies

Brownies

1 cup sugar

½ cup shortening

2 eggs

2 tablespoons cocoa

1 teaspoon vanilla extract

¾ cup flour

½ cup chopped pecans

Cream sugar and Crisco together. Mix in eggs, cocoa, flour and vanilla. Pour into a greased 8x8-inch pan. Top with pecans and bake at 350° for 30 minutes.

thinkstock / istockphoto / gabrieldome

Oatmeal Peanut Butter Bars with Chocolate Chips

1 stick butter, softened

½ cup sugar

½ cup brown sugar

⅓ cup peanut butter

1 egg, beaten

1 cup flour

1 cup quick oats

½ teaspoon baking soda

¼ teaspoon salt

1 cup chocolate chips

Glaze

½ cup powdered sugar

¼ cup peanut butter

1 to 2 tablespoons milk

Combine all ingredients, except chocolate chips. Bake at 350° in a 9x13-inch pan for 20 minutes. After removing from oven, immediately top with chocolate chips. While chocolate melts, mix glaze ingredients and drizzle over chocolate. Blend chocolate and glaze with a spatula. Cool before cutting (if you can resist the temptation) and enjoy.

Cookies

thinkstock / istockphoto / Bob Ingelhart

Pineapple Brownies

2 eggs

1 (20-ounce) can crushed pineapple, drained

1 teaspoon baking soda

1¾ cups flour

1¾ cups sugar or brown sugar

Mix all ingredients together. Pour into greased and floured cookie sheet. Bake at 350° for 25 minutes.

Almond Butterscotch Bars

1 cup butter, softened

¾ cup light brown sugar

1 teaspoon vanilla extract

½ teaspoon almond extract

½ teaspoon salt

2 cups flour

1 cup butterscotch morsels

1 cup silvered almonds

Cream together butter and sugar; beat in vanilla, almond extract and salt. Gradually beat in flour until well blended. Press mixture into 9x13-inch pan. Sprinkle butterscotch morsels and silvered almonds over mixture and press lightly. Bake at 350° about 20 minutes or until golden brown. Cool and cut into squares.

Congo Squares

1 (16-ounce) box light brown sugar

½ cup oil

3 eggs

3 cups self-rising flour

1 cup pecans

1 teaspoon vanilla flavoring

1 (6-ounce) package chocolate chips

Mix all and bake at 350° for 30 minutes. Cool and cut into squares.

Gooey Cookie Bars

½ cup butter

1½ cups crushed graham cracker crumbs

1 (14-ounce) can sweetened condensed milk

1 cup coconut flakes

1 cup chocolate chips

1 cup chopped almonds

Preheat oven to 350°. Place butter in a 9x9-inch square pan in oven to melt (or quickly melt in microwave). Sprinkle graham cracker crumbs over melted butter. Carefully pour condensed milk over crumbs covering all. Sprinkle coconut, chocolate chips and nuts over top. Bake 25 to 30 minutes. Cool in pan before cutting into bars.

Rice Crispy Treats

3 tablespoons butter

1 (10-ounce) package JET-PUFFED marshmallows

5½ cups Rice Krispies cereal

Melt butter in large saucepan over low heat. Add marshmallows; stir until fully melted. Remove from heat. Immediately add cereal; mix lightly until well coated. Press firmly into lightly greased 9x13-inch pan. Cool completely; cut into squares.

Peanut Butter Rice Crispy Treats

1 stick margarine

1 cup sugar

1½ cups light corn syrup

1½ cups crunchy peanut butter

1 (10-ounce) box Rice Krispies cereal

In a large saucepan over medium-low heat, warm first 4 ingredients until hot and bubbly. Add cereal and mix well. Pour in a treated 9x13-inch pan. Press to bottom of pan. Cut into squares when cool.

Heavenly Hash

12 large marshmallows

1 pound milk chocolate

1 cup chopped nuts

Dice marshmallows. Boil water in bottom of a double boiler. Turn off heat. Place milk chocolate in top of double boiler. Stir occasionally until melted. Line a cookie sheet with wax paper. Pour in ½ melted chocolate. Cover evenly with marshmallows and nuts. Pour remaining chocolate over top. Cool before cutting into squares.

Cheese Fudge

2 cups butter

1 pound processed cheese, cubed

4 (1-pound) packages powdered sugar

1 cup cocoa powder

1 tablespoon vanilla extract

4 tablespoons chopped peanuts

In a large saucepan, melt butter over low heat; add cheese and stir until well blended. Add powdered sugar and cocoa. Stir in vanilla and nuts. Spread on cookie sheets lined with foil. Refrigerate until set. Cut and serve.

Rocky Road Fudge

2 cups semisweet chocolate morsels

1 (14-ounce) can sweetened condensed milk

1 teaspoon vanilla extract

3 cups miniature marshmallows

1½ cups coarsely chopped walnuts

Line a 9x13-inch baking pan with foil. Lightly grease foil. Microwave morsels and condensed milk on high 1 minute; stir. Microwave at additional 10 to 20 second intervals, stirring until mixture is smooth. Stir in vanilla. Fold in marshmallows and nuts. Press mixture into baking pan. Refrigerate until ready to serve.

thinkstock / istockphoto / Svetlana Kolpakova

Peanut Butter Fudge

⅔ cup evaporated milk

2 cups sugar

1 cup crunchy peanut butter

1 teaspoon vanilla extract

1 cup marshmallow crème

In a saucepan, stir milk and sugar together until well blended. Cook over medium heat until a drop in cold water forms a soft ball (234° to 240° on a candy thermometer). Remove from heat. Stir in peanut butter, vanilla and marshmallow crème. Beat until smooth. Spread in buttered rectangular pan, about 9x13-inch. Cool and cut into squares.

Imitation Butterfingers

1 (16-ounce) jar crunchy peanut butter

1 (16-ounce) box original Wheat Thins

1 (24-ounce) package chocolate almond bark

Make sandwiches with peanut butter and Wheat Thins. Melt chocolate bark in microwave. Dip sandwiches in chocolate until covered completely. Place on wax paper to cool.

Pretzel Turtles

20 mini pretzels

20 chocolate-covered caramel candies

20 pecan halves

Preheat oven to 300°. Arrange pretzels in a single layer on parchment-lined cookie sheet. Place 1 chocolate-covered caramel candy on each pretzel. Bake 4 minutes. Remove from oven and while candy is still warm, press a pecan half onto each candy-covered pretzel. Cool completely before storing in an airtight container.

Millionaires

4 tablespoons milk

1 (24-ounce) package caramels

3 cups chopped pecans

1 bar paraffin

1 (12-ounce) package semisweet chocolate morsels

Combine milk and caramels in a large saucepan and cook over low heat until caramels are melted. Stir in pecans. Drop by teaspoons onto greased cookie sheet. Place in freezer until solid. Melt paraffin and chocolate pieces in saucepan over low heat. Dip each caramel piece in chocolate mixture. Store in a dry place.

Microwave Pralines

1 pound light brown sugar

½ pint whipping cream

2 cups chopped pecans

2 tablespoons margarine

In a 4-quart mixing bowl, microwave brown sugar and whipping cream 9 minutes without stirring. Remove from microwave; add pecans and margarine. Drop by spoonfuls onto buttered wax paper. Allow to cool before serving.

Praline Caramel Candy

4 cups sugar

2 cups half-and-half

¼ teaspoon salt

2 cups chopped pecans

In a saucepan, mix 3 cups of the sugar, all the half-and-half and salt together until the sugar is partially dissolved. Cook slowly on low heat until sugar is completely dissolved. Meanwhile, in a large skillet, slowly brown the remaining cup of sugar. Stirring constantly, carefully add the half-and-half and sugar mixture to the caramelized sugar in the skillet. Cook over medium heat until a drop in cold water forms a soft ball (234° to 240° on a candy thermometer). Beat, then stir in the pecans. Drop by teaspoonfuls onto wax paper.

Easy Peanut Brittle

1 cup sugar

½ cup light corn syrup

1 cup raw peanuts

Dash salt

1 teaspoon vanilla extract

1 teaspoon margarine

1 teaspoon baking soda

Mix sugar, corn syrup, peanuts and salt in microwaveable mixing bowl. Cook on high 5 minutes; stir. Cook on high 3 minutes. Add vanilla and margarine; stir to combine. Cook 2 minutes. Stir in baking soda. Spread on greased baking sheet. Cool and break into pieces.

thinkstock / istockphoto / Shane Thompson

White Crunch

2 cups Rice Krispies

2 cups Cap'n Crunch cereal

2 cups mini marshmallows

2 cups pecan pieces

1 (24-ounce) package vanilla almond bark

Mix all ingredients except almond bark in a large bowl. Melt almond bark and pour immediately over mixture. Mix well and quickly spoon bite-size balls onto wax paper.

Mrs. Vicki's Cornflake Candy

1 cup light corn syrup

1 cup sugar

1 teaspoon vanilla extract

1¼ cups creamy peanut butter

5 cups cornflakes

In a saucepan, cook corn syrup and sugar over low heat, stirring constantly, until mixture comes to a full rolling boil. Remove from heat. Stir in vanilla and peanut butter, mixing until creamy. Mix in cornflakes 1 cup at a time. Drop by spoonfuls onto wax paper. Allow to cool.

Spraying your measuring cup with non-stick spray before filling it with peanut butter helps the peanut butter slide out more easily; you can also fill the cup with scalding hot water, empty water then measure the peanut butter.

Caramel Cereal Bars

3 cups Rice Krispies

2 cups cornflakes

1 cup peanuts

1 (14-ounce) package caramels

2 tablespoons water

Lightly grease a 9x13-inch baking dish. In a large bowl, combine cereals and peanuts. In microwave-safe bowl, combine caramels and water. Microwave on medium 3 to 5 minutes or until caramels are melted. Pour over cereal mixture and mix well. Press into greased pan. Chill 1 hour or until firm. Cut into squares.

thinkstock / istockphoto / Warren Price

Haystacks

1 (12-ounce) package butterscotch chips

1 (5-ounce) can chow mein noodles

1 cup cocktail peanuts

Microwave morsels 1 minute; stir. Continue microwaving in 20 second intervals, stirring each time, until morsels are melted and smooth. Add chow mein noodles and nuts; stir quickly and thoroughly until noodles are evenly coated. Working quickly, drop by tablespoon onto wax paper.

Cookie Dough Truffles

1 stick (½ cup) butter, softened

¾ cup packed brown sugar

1 teaspoon vanilla extract

2 cups all-purpose flour

1 (14-ounce) can sweetened condensed milk

½ cup miniature semisweet chocolate chips

½ cup chopped walnuts, optional

1½ pounds dark chocolate candy coating

Cream butter and brown sugar until light and fluffy. Beat in vanilla. Gradually add flour, alternately with milk, beating well after each addition. Stir in chocolate chips and walnuts. Shape into 1-inch balls; place on wax paper-lined baking sheets. Loosely cover and refrigerate 1 to 2 hours or until firm. Melt candy coating per package directions; stir until smooth. Dip balls in coating; allow excess to drip off. Place on wax paper-lined baking sheets. Refrigerate until firm, about 15 minutes. Store in refrigerator.

Date Loaf Candy

3 cups sugar

1 cup milk

1 (8-ounce) package pitted dates, chopped

1 tablespoon butter

1 cup chopped pecans

Mix sugar and milk in saucepan. Bring to a boil and add dates. Boil slowly until a drop in cold water forms a soft ball (234° to 240° on a candy thermometer). Stir in butter and set saucepan in a pan of cold water. When cool, beat until thick. Add nuts. Pour into a dampened dishcloth and shape into a roll. Chill; slice when cold.

Potato Chip Candy

9 ounces white baking chocolate, melted

2 cups crushed potato chips

½ cup chopped pecans

Melt white chocolate in microwave following package directions. Lightly stir in potato chips and pecans. Drop by tablespoonfuls onto wax paper-lined baking sheets. Refrigerate until set.

Granny's Divinity

2 egg whites

½ cup water

2½ cups sugar

½ cup light corn syrup

1 cup chopped pecans

Beat egg whites in a glass bowl until stiff. In a saucepan, mix water, sugar and corn syrup together; cook until a drop in cold water forms a soft ball (234° to 240° on a candy thermometer). Beat less than half of the sugar mixture into the egg whites. Return rest of sugar mixture to stove and heat until a drop in cold water forms a rigid ball (250° to 265° on a candy thermometer). Add to egg whites and beat until it loses its gloss. Mix in pecans. Working quickly, drop spoonfuls onto wax paper.

thinkstock / istockphoto / Vassiliy Vassilenko

Popcorn Balls

½ cup sugar

¼ cup margarine

½ cup light corn syrup

½ teaspoon salt

8 cups popped popcorn

Put all ingredients, except popcorn, in a Dutch oven over medium heat. Stir constantly until mixture reaches soft-ball stage (240° on a candy thermometer or when a small amount dropped in cold water forms a soft ball). Stir in popcorn, stirring constantly until well coated. Cool about 3½ minutes. Dip hands into cool water and shape mixture into 2-inch balls. Place on wax paper until cool and then wrap in plastic wrap. Makes about 10 balls.

Strawberry Kisses

1 (8-ounce) package cream cheese

1 cup sugar

2 pounds whole strawberries

1 cup finely chopped pecans

Heat cream cheese in microwave until melted, about 1 minute. Add sugar; stir until creamy. Hold strawberries by stem end and dip in cream cheese mixture. Roll in pecans. Serve immediately or chill until ready to serve. Serve with toothpicks.

Cranberry Casserole

3 medium apples (Gala or other flavorful baking apples)

2 cups fresh cranberries

½ to ¾ cup sugar

Topping:

1 cup quick oats

⅓ cup self-rising flour

½ cup brown sugar

1 cup chopped pecans

1 stick butter, melted

Peel, core and slice apples. Put into buttered 9x13-inch dish. Place cranberries on top of apples. Sprinkle sugar over mixture. For topping, mix oats, flour, brown sugar and pecans in zip-close bag. Add melted butter and shake well. Crumble over apple mixture. Bake at 350° for 30 minutes. Uncover and bake 30 minutes longer.

Chocolate Bread Pudding

2 cups milk

6 slices white bread, crusts trimmed

½ cup sugar

⅓ cup cocoa powder

2 eggs, separated

2 tablespoons butter, melted

1 teaspoon vanilla extract

½ cup semisweet chocolate chunks

Whipped cream

Cocoa powder

Heat milk in a large saucepan just until tiny bubbles form; remove from heat. Cube bread and add to milk; stir until bread is soaked. Add sugar, cocoa and egg yolks; stir until well blended. Add butter and vanilla; set aside. Beat egg whites until stiff peaks form; fold into mixture along with chocolate chunks. Pour into 6 lightly greased custard cups. Set cups in large pan filled with 1 inch hot water. Bake at 350° for 40 minutes or until firm. Serve warm or cold garnished with whipped cream and cocoa powder.

Donna's Best Bread Pudding

2 cups sugar

5 large eggs, beaten

2 cups milk

2 teaspoons vanilla extract

3 cups cubed Hawaiian bread, allow to sit overnight in a bowl

1 cup packed light brown sugar

¼ cup (half stick) butter, softened

1 cup chopped pecans

Preheat the oven to 350°. Grease a 9x13-inch pan. Mix together sugar, eggs and milk in a bowl; add vanilla. Pour over cubed bread and let sit 10 minutes. In another bowl, mix together until crumbly the brown sugar, butter and pecans. Pour bread mixture into prepared pan. Sprinkle brown sugar mixture over the top and bake 35 to 45 minutes or until set. Remove from oven.

Sauce

1 cup sugar

1 stick butter, melted

1 egg, beaten

2 teaspoons vanilla extract

¼ cup brandy

In a saucepan, mix together the sugar, butter, egg and vanilla. Cook over medium heat, stirring until sugar is melted. Add the brandy, stirring well. Pour over bread pudding. Serve warm or cold.

Hot Fruit

¾ cup brown sugar

½ stick margarine, melted

1 teaspoon cinnamon

1 (15.25-ounce) can sliced peaches

1 (15.25-ounce) can sliced pears

1 (20-ounce) can pineapple chunks

1 (15-ounce) can mandarin oranges

1 (10-ounce) jar maraschino cherries

Combine brown sugar, margarine and cinnamon. Drain all fruits. Combine with sugar mixture. Pour into treated 3-quart baking dish and bake 1½ hours at 375°.

Warm Fruit Compote

2 (29-ounce) cans sliced peaches, drained

2 (29-ounce) cans pear halves, sliced and drained

1 (20-ounce) can pineapple slices, drained

1 (15-ounce) can apricot halves, sliced and drained

1 (21-ounce) can cherry pie filling

In a crockpot combine peaches, pears, pineapple and apricots. Top with pie filling. Cover and cook on high 2 to 2½ hours or until hot throughout. Serve hot or cold.

Other Desserts

Apple Dessert

3 large baking apples

1 tablespoon butter, melted

1 tablespoon lemon juice

1½ tablespoons brown sugar

½ teaspoon cinnamon

Core and peel apples. Cut into eighths. Place in crockpot. Drizzle butter and lemon juice over apples. Sprinkle sugar and cinnamon on top. Cover and cook on low 3 hours or on high 1½ hours.

Mrs. Vicki's Apple Dumplings

2 Granny Smith apples, peeled and cored

2 (8-count) cans crescent rolls

2 sticks butter, no substitute

2 cups sugar

1 teaspoon vanilla extract

Cinnamon

1 (8-ounce) can Mountain Dew

Slice apples in eighths. Wrap each slice in a crescent roll. Place in a greased 11x13-inch baking dish. Melt butter; add sugar and vanilla and stir well. Pour over apples. Sprinkle with cinnamon. Pour entire can of Mountain Dew over top. Bake at 350° for 40 minutes. Best served warm with vanilla ice cream.

I had never eaten Apple Dumplings before I met my husband. His Mom served these the first time I met her, and I request them for every holiday.

Other Desserts

Rice Pudding

3 cups cooked rice

½ stick butter, melted

1 cup raisins

½ teaspoon nutmeg

3 eggs, well beaten

½ cup milk

1½ cups sugar

Mix all ingredients together. Pour in treated 2-quart baking dish. Bake at 350° for 30 minutes or until top is lightly browned.

Crockpot Custard

2 cups whole milk

3 eggs, lightly beaten

⅓ cup plus ½ teaspoon sugar, divided use

1 teaspoon vanilla extract

¼ teaspoon cinnamon

Heat milk in a small saucepan until skin forms on top; remove from heat and slightly cool. Meanwhile, in a large mixing bowl combine eggs, ⅓ cup sugar and vanilla. Slowly stir cooled milk into egg mixture. Pour into a greased 1-quart baking dish that will fit inside the crockpot. Mix cinnamon and ½ teaspoon reserved sugar in a small bowl. Sprinkle over custard mixture. Cover with foil and place in crockpot. Pour hot water to a depth of 1 inch around dish in crockpot. Cover and cook on high 2 to 3 hours or until custard is set. Serve warm.

Granny's Famous Egg Custard

3 cups milk

1½ cups sugar

Pinch salt

½ stick margarine

4 teaspoons vanilla extract

5 eggs, beaten

Nutmeg

Preheat oven to 450°. In a saucepan, mix all ingredients except eggs and nutmeg. Heat mixture to a hard boil. Beat eggs well and add to hot mixture then immediately pour into a 4-quart casserole dish. Sprinkle with nutmeg. Bake 10 minutes then reduce heat to 350° and bake 10 minutes longer or until a table knife comes out clean when inserted in center.

Granny was known for her egg custard. Everyone around loved it! If you came to visit Granny, you would more than likely leave with her egg custard recipe and a pie!

thinkstock / istockphoto / raul taborda

Other Desserts

Chocolate Gravy

¼ cup cocoa powder

3 tablespoons all-purpose flour

¾ cup sugar

2 cups milk

1 tablespoon butter, softened

2 teaspoons vanilla extract

Whisk the cocoa, flour and sugar together in a bowl until there are no lumps. Add milk and whisk until well incorporated. Transfer mixture to a saucepan and cook over medium heat, stirring frequently, until it thickens, 7 to 10 minutes. Remove from heat and add the butter and vanilla, stirring until butter is melted. Serve immediately over plain cupcakes, sliced pound cake, or even left-over biscuits.

Pineapple Casserole

6 slices white bread, torn into small pieces

1 (20-ounce) can crushed pineapple, drained

3 eggs, beaten

2 cups sugar

½ cup butter, melted

Mix all ingredients; pour into a greased 2-quart baking dish. Bake at 350° for 30 minutes.

Other Desserts

Pineapple Pudding

1 (20-ounce) can crushed pineapple, undrained

¼ cup water

2 eggs, beaten

2 tablespoons cornstarch

½ to ¾ cup sugar

Combine all ingredients inside a crockpot. Cook on high, covered, for ½ hour and then on low 3½ hours.

Granny's Sweet Stuff

1 (15.25-ounce) can crushed pineapple, drained

1 (14-ounce) can sweetened condensed milk

1 (8-ounce) carton whipped topping

1 (21-ounce) can pie filling (your choice)

Mix all ingredients together. Refrigerate until cold.

Banana Split Dessert

2 cups crushed graham crackers

6 tablespoons butter, melted

2 cups plus 6 tablespoons powdered sugar

2 egg whites

1 stick butter, softened

3 to 5 bananas

1 (20-ounce) can crushed pineapple, drained

1 (8-ounce) carton whipped topping

1 cup chopped pecans

1 cup chopped cherries

1 (24-ounce) bottle chocolate syrup

Combine graham crackers, melted butter and 6 tablespoons powdered sugar to make crust. Press in bottom of square 2-quart casserole dish. Combine 2 cups powdered sugar, egg whites and butter; beat 10 minutes. Pour over crust. Slice bananas lengthwise; place over top of powdered sugar mixture. Spread pineapple over bananas then spread whipped topping over pineapple. Top with pecans and cherries. Refrigerate 2 hours or until ready to serve. Drizzle syrup over top just before serving.

When you get home from the store; separate bananas from the main stem. They will not ripen as quickly. And to avoid having strings on a banana when you peel it, take the peel off from the bottom — the primates do it that way.

Simple Banana Pudding

**1 large (5.1-ounce) box instant vanilla pudding mix,
plus ingredients to prepare**

1 (14-ounce) can sweetened condensed milk

1 (12-ounce) carton whipped topping

10 bananas, sliced

1 (12-ounce) box vanilla wafers

Prepare pudding according to directions on the box. Mix in condensed milk and whipped topping. Layer wafers in bottom of 3-quart casserole. Cover wafers with ⅓ pudding and ½ bananas. Add another layer wafers, ⅓ pudding and ½ bananas. End with remaining pudding. Refrigerate overnight before serving.

Tapioca

2 quarts whole milk

1¼ cups sugar

1 cup dry small pearl tapioca

4 eggs

1 teaspoon vanilla extract

Whipped topping (optional)

Combine milk and sugar in crockpot, stirring until sugar is dissolved. Stir in tapioca. Cover and cook on high 3 hours. In a small bowl, lightly beat eggs. Beat in vanilla and 1 cup hot milk from slow cooker. When well mixed, stir into crockpot. Cover and cook on high 20 minutes. Chill. Serve with whipped topping.

Snickers Mousse Dessert

3 cups crushed graham crackers

½ cup butter, melted

1 large (5.9-ounce) box instant chocolate pudding

2 cups milk

2 cups whipped topping

2 tablespoons chunky peanut butter, softened

Combine cracker crackers butter; press into bottom of 9x13-inch pan. Combine pudding mix and milk until well blended. Mix in whipped topping and peanut butter. Pour over crackers and refrigerate until set.

Yalis' Strawberry Trifle

1 store-bought angel food cake

1 large (5.1-ounce) box vanilla instant pudding

1 cup milk

2 pounds fresh strawberries

1 (12-ounce) carton whipped topping

Crumble cake into a large, clear punch bowl. Combine dry pudding mix with 1 cup milk; beat 2 minutes. Refrigerate to set. Meanwhile, slice strawberries and, if not sweet enough, stir in a little sugar; set aside until ready to assemble trifle. When pudding is set, spoon it over cake, top with strawberries then whipped topping. Refrigerate until ready to serve.

My husband's Aunt Yalis lives in Florida. She rarely comes down to good ole Mississippi, but when she does, she always brings her Strawberry Trifle. The kids love it!

Red Velvet Moon Pies

1 box red velvet cake mix

1 stick butter, softened

2 eggs, beaten

1 (15-ounce) can cream cheese frosting

Mix dry cake mix, butter and eggs until well combined. Drop by teaspoonfuls onto a cookie sheet lined with parchment paper, and then flatten each cookie. Bake at 350° for 8 to 10 minutes. Cool; spread cream cheese icing between 2 cookies and press together. Repeat until all cookies are used.

thinkstock / istockphoto / Stephanie Frey

Dirt Dessert

1 (16-ounce) package Oreos

1 (8-ounce) package cream cheese, softened

4 tablespoons butter, softened

1 cup powdered sugar

2 (3.4-ounce) packages instant vanilla pudding mix

3½ cups cold milk

1 (12-ounce) carton whipped topping

1 new flower pot

Silk flowers

Candy gummy worms

Crush cookies until fine. Set aside. In a mixing bowl, beat cream cheese, butter and sugar until smooth. In a separate bowl, mix pudding and milk; beat 2 minutes until thick. Combine with cream cheese mixture. Mix in whipped topping. Line flower pot with foil and alternate layers of crushed cookies and pudding, ending with cookies. Chill overnight. Decorate with silk flowers and gummy worms.

Oreo Frozen Peanut Butter Dessert

30 Oreo cookies, finely crushed

3 tablespoons butter, melted

1 cup peanut butter, softened

1¾ quarts vanilla ice cream, softened

1 (8-ounce) carton whipped topping

6 (1-ounce) squares semisweet baking chocolate

½ cup peanuts, chopped

Mix cookie crumbs and butter. Press into bottom of 9x13-inch pan. Place in freezer. Microwave peanut butter. Swirl peanut butter into ice cream. Spread over crust. Freeze 30 minutes. Place whipped topping and chocolate in a bowl and microwave 2 minutes; stir to combine. Spread whipped topping mixture over ice cream. Top with nuts. Freeze 4 hours.

Blueberry Ice Cream

2 cups fresh blueberries

¾ cup sugar

⅛ teaspoon salt

2 eggs

1 cup milk

1 pint heavy cream

In a saucepan over medium heat begin to crush the blueberries with the sugar and salt until the juices come to a slow boil. Reduce the heat to a low simmer and continue to stir and crush the mixture for about 5 minutes as it cools. Whisk the eggs together until smooth, about 1 to 2 minutes, and add to the blueberry juices and blend (if you are worried about raw eggs, try to get them into the mix while the temperature is still above 180° but not while boiling). Pour mixture into a blender container and add the milk. Blend until smooth. Cover; place in the refrigerator (not the freezer) overnight. In the morning, pour mixture into a larger bowl and add the heavy cream. Stir gently, only enough to blend. Pour into an ice cream maker and freeze according to manufacturer's directions.

Other Desserts

A Little Something Extra...

The following pages contain helpful information I've found to be valuable in my own kitchen. You will find a list of common Measurement Equivalents and Pan Sizes by Volume. So, if you can't find your ⅛ cup measure; no problem, just use 2 tablespoons instead. With the list of ingredient equivalents you will know if a recipe calls for 2 cups chocolate chips, a 12-ounce package is just the right size. Common substitutions and a list of the approximate volume for various pan sizes will provide even more good help. While much of this information will be great for the recipes in Family Favorite Recipes, *this list is meant to be useful well beyond the pages of this cookbook. Enjoy!*

Measurement Equivalents

1 tablespoon = 3 teaspoons

1/16 cup = 1 tablespoon

⅛ cup = 2 tablespoons = 1 ounce

¼ cup = 4 tablespoons = 2 ounces

⅓ cup = 5 tablespoons + 1 teaspoon

½ cup = 8 tablespoons = 4 ounces

⅔ cup = 10 tablespoons + 2 teaspoons

¾ cup = 12 tablespoons

1 cup = 48 teaspoons = 16 tablespoons = 8 ounces

1 pint = 2 cups = 16 ounces

1 quart = 2 pints = 4 cups = 32 ounces

1 gallon = 4 quarts

1 pound (dry) = 16 ounces

Pan Sizes by Volume

½ cup
Muffin or cupcake pan each cup

4 cups
9-inch pie pan
8-inch round cake pan
11-inch road tart pan
Small loaf pan (4x8x2¾-inch)

6 cups
9-inch round cake pan
Bundt pan (7½x3-inch)
9-inch deep dish pie pan
7x11x2-inch rectangular pan

8 cups
8x8x2-inch square pan
9x9x1½-inch square pan
Large loaf pan (9x5x3-inch)

9 cups
Bundt pan (9x3-inch)
Tube pan (8x3-inch)

10 cups
9x9x2-inch square pan
9x13-inch rectangular pan
Jelly roll pan (10½x15½x1-inch pan)
Springform pan (9x2½-inch)

12 cups
Jelly roll pan (17½x12½x1-inch pan)
10-inch square
Tube pan (9x3-inch)
Bundt pan (10x3½-inch)
Springform pan (9x3-inch)
Springform pan (10x2½-inch)

14 cups
9x13x2-inch rectangular pan

16 cups
Jelly roll pan (15½x10½x1-inch pan)
Tube pan (10x4-inch)

Ingredient Equivalents

Apples:
1 pound = 3 medium or 3 cups sliced

Bananas:
1 pound = 3 medium or 1⅓ cups mashed

Barley:
1 cup raw quick-cooking = about 3 cups cooked

Beans:
1 cup dry = 2 to 2½ cups cooked

Blueberries:
1 pint = 2½ cups

Bread:
1 pound loaf = 16 regular or 28 thin slices

Bread crumbs:
½ cup fresh = 1 slice bread with crust

Butter or margarine:
1 stick = ½ cup or 8 tablespoons or 4 ounces

Cabbage:
1 pound = 4 to 5 cups coarsely chopped

Celery:
1 medium-size bunch = about 4 cups chopped

Cheese:
4 ounces = 1 cup shredded

Cherries:
1 pound = about 2 cups pitted

Chicken:
2½- to 3-pound fryer = 2½ cups diced cooked meat

Chocolate:
1 ounce unsweetened or semisweet = 1 square

Chocolate chips:
6-ounce package = 1 cup

Cocoa:
8-ounce can unsweetened = 2 cups

Cornmeal:
1 cup raw = about 4 cups cooked

Cottage cheese:
8 ounces = 1 cup

Couscous:
1 cup raw = about 2½ cups cooked

Cranberries:
12-ounce bag = 3 cups

Cream:
1 cup heavy or whipping = 2 cups whipped

Cream cheese:
8-ounce package = 1 cup
3-ounce package = 6 tablespoons

Egg white:
1 large = about 2 tablespoons

Egg yolk:
1 large = about 1½ tablespoons

Flour:
1 pound all-purpose = about 3½ cups

Gelatin:
1 envelope unflavored = 2½ teaspoons

Gingersnaps:
15 cookies = about 1 cup crumbs

Graham crackers:
7 whole crackers = 1 cup crumbs

Grits:
1 cup uncooked = about 4½ cups cooked

Honey:
16 ounces = 1⅓ cups

Lemon:
1 medium = about 3 tablespoons juice
and 1 tablespoon grated peel

Lentils:
1 cup uncooked = about 2½ cups cooked

Macaroni, elbow:
1 cup uncooked = about 2 cups cooked

Milk, condensed:
14-ounce can = 1¼ cups

Milk, evaporated:
5-ounce can = ⅔ cup

Molasses:
12 ounces = 1½ cups

Noodles:
8 ounces uncooked medium
= about 4 cups cooked

Nuts:
4 ounces = 1 cup chopped

Oats:
1 cup raw old-fashioned or quick-cooking
= about 2 cups cooked

Onion:
1 large = 1 cup chopped

Orange:
1 medium = ⅓ to ½ cup juice
and 2 tablespoons grated peel

Peaches:
1 pound = about 3 medium or 2½ cups sliced

Pears:
1 pound = about 3 medium or 2¼ cups sliced

Peppers:
1 large bell = about 1 cup chopped

Pineapple:
1 large = about 4 cups cubed

Popcorn:
¼ cup unpopped = about 4 cups popped

Potatoes:
1 pound all-purpose = about 3 medium
or 3 cups sliced or 2 cups mashed

Raisins:
15-ounce box = about 2 cups

Raspberries:
½ pint = about 1 cup

Rice:
1 cup uncooked regular = about 3 cups cooked
1 cup uncooked instant = about 2 cups cooked

Saltine crackers:
28 squares = about 1 cup crumbs

Shortening:
1 pound = 2½ cups

Sour cream:
8 ounces = 1 cup

Spaghetti:
8 ounces uncooked = about 4 cups cooked

Split peas:
1 cup raw = about 2½ cups cooked

Strawberries:
1 pound = about 3¼ cups whole
or 2½ cups sliced

Sugar:
1 pound confectioners' = 3¾ cups
1 pound granulated = 2¼ to 2½ cups
1 pound light or dark brown
= 2¼ cups packed

Tomatoes:
1 pound = 3 medium

Vanilla wafers:
30 cookies = 1 cup crumbs

Yeast:
1 package active dry = 2½ teaspoons

Ingredient Substitutions

Bacon:
1 slice cooked bacon = 1 tablespoon bacon bits

Baking powder:
1 teaspoon baking powder = ½ teaspoon cream of tartar plus ¼ teaspoon baking soda

Broth:
1 cup chicken or beef broth = 1 bouillon cube or 1 envelope
or 1 teaspoon instant bouillon plus 1 cup boiling water

Buttermilk:
1 cup buttermilk = 1 tablespoon vinegar or lemon juice plus enough milk to equal 1 cup.
Let stand 5 minutes to thicken. Or use 1 cup plain yogurt

Chives:
Use green onion tops

Chocolate:
1 ounce unsweetened chocolate = 3 tablespoons unsweetened cocoa powder
plus 1 tablespoon butter, margarine, or oil
6 ounces semisweet chocolate = 1 cup chocolate chips
or 6 tablespoons unsweetened cocoa powder
plus 7 tablespoons sugar and 4 tablespoons butter, margarine, or oil

Cornstarch (for thickening):
1 tablespoon cornstarch = 2 tablespoons flour or 2 tablespoons quick-cooking tapioca

Fish sauce, Asian:
1 tablespoon fish sauce = 2 teaspoons soy sauce plus 1 teaspoon anchovy paste

Flour:
1 cup cake flour = 1 cup minus 2 tablespoons sifted all-purpose flour
1 cup self-rising flour = 1 cup all-purpose flour
plus ¼ teaspoon baking powder and a pinch of salt

Heavy cream (for cooking, not whipping):
1 cup heavy cream = ⅓ cup butter plus ¾ cup milk

Milk:
1 cup whole milk = ½ cup evaporated milk plus ½ cup water

Pancetta:
Use sliced smoked bacon simmered in water for 3 minutes, then rinsed and drained

Pepper, ground red:
⅛ teaspoon red pepper = 4 drops hot-pepper sauce

Pine nuts:
Use walnuts or almonds

Prosciutto:
Use ham, preferably Westphalian or a country ham, such as Smithfield

Shallots:
Use red onion

Sour cream:
1 cup sour cream = 1 cup plain yogurt (in unheated recipe). To prevent yogurt from curdling in a cooked recipe, you will have to stabilize it with 1 egg white or 1 tablespoon of cornstarch or flour dissolved in a little cold water for every quart of yogurt

Sugar:
1 cup light brown sugar = 1 cup granulated sugar plus 1 tablespoon molasses
or 1 cup dark brown sugar

Tartar Sauce:
1 cup tartar sauce = 6 tablespoons mayonnaise plus 2 tablespoons pickle relish

Tomato juice:
1 cup tomato juice = ½ cup tomato sauce plus ½ cup water

Tomato sauce:
15-ounce can tomato sauce = 6-ounce can tomato paste plus 1½ cans water

Vanilla extract:
Use brandy or an appropriately flavored liqueur

Vegetable oil:
1 cup vegetable oil = ½ pound (2 sticks) butter

Whipping cream (whipped):
1 cup whipped whipping cream = 6 to 8 ounces Cool Whip

Yeast:
1 package active dry yeast = ½-ounce yeast cake
or 1 package quick-rise yeast (allow half the rising time for quick rise)

Yogurt:
1 cup plain yogurt = 1 cup buttermilk

Index

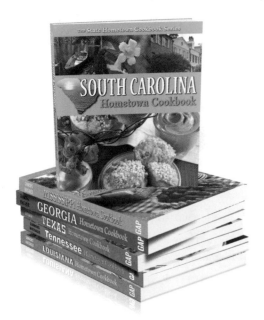

State Hometown Cookbook Series

A Hometown Taste of America, One State at a Time

EACH: $18.95 • 248 - 272 pp • 8x9
paperbound • full-color photos

Includes:
Georgia Hometown Cookbook
Louisiana Hometown Cookbook
Mississippi Hometown Cookbook
South Carolina Hometown Cookbook
Tennessee Hometown Cookbook
Texas Hometown Cookbook
Coming soon...
West Virginia Hometown Cookbook

State Back Road Restaurants Cookbook Series

Every Road Leads to Delicious Food

EACH: $18.95 • 248 - 272 pp • 6x9
paperbound • full-color photos

Includes:
Alabama Back Road Restaurant Recipes
Kentucky Back Road Restaurant Recipes

Eat & Explore State Cookbook Series

Discover the USA Like You've Never Tasted it Before

EACH: $18.95 • 248 - 272 pp • 7x9
paperbound • full-color photos

Includes:
Eat & Explore Arkansas
Eat & Explore Minnesota
Eat & Explore Oklahoma
Eat & Explore Virginia
Eat & Explore Washington

Great American Publishers • *Everyday Recipes for the Everyday Cook*
www.GreatAmericanPublishers.com • toll-free 1.888.854.5954

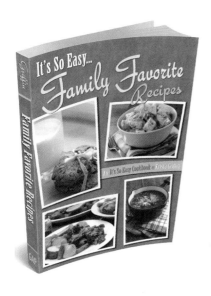

Makes a Great Gift!

ORDER ONLINE AT:

www.CookbookADay.com

ALSO AVAILABLE ONLINE:
- Free Recipes
- Videos
- Cooking Hints & Tips
- Free Sample Cookbooks

CALL TOLL-FREE

1.888.854.5954
to order or to request a free catalog about

Great American Cookbooks

Order Form

	Qty	Amount
Family Favorite Recipes • $18.95		
Game for All Seasons • $16.95		
State Hometown Cookbook Series:		
Georgia • $18.95		
Louisiana • $18.95		
Mississippi • $18.95		
South Carolina • $18.95		
Tennessee • $18.95		
Texas • $18.95		

	Qty	Amount
Eat & Explore State Cookbook Series:		
Arkansas • $18.95		
Minnesota • $18.95		
Oklahoma • $18.95		
Virginia • $18.95		
Washington • $18.95		
State Back Road Restaurants Series:		
Alabama • $18.95		
Kentucky • $18.95		

Name _____

Address _____

_____

Phone _____

Email _____

Shipping is $3 1st book: $1 each additional; more than 4 books = FREE shipping

Subtotal	_____
Shipping	_____
Total	_____

Mail Check or Money Order to:
Great American Publishers
P. O. Box 1305 - Kosciusko, MS 39090
Call 1.888.854.5954 to order by credit card
Order online www.CookbookADay.com